WINERIES OF INDIANA

A Guide to the Wineries and Vineyards of Indiana

D. L. Tadevich

INDIANA WINERIES

NORTHERN INDIANA
1. Anderson Orchard and Winery
2. Dune Ridge Winery
3. Lake Michigan Winery
4. Satek Winery

CENTRAL INDIANA
5. Easley's Winery
6. Gaia Winery
7. Chateau Thomas Winery
8. Terre Vin Winery
9. Ferrin's Fruit Winery
10. Wilson Winery

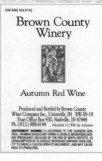

SOUTH CENTRAL INDIANA
11. Oliver Winery and Vineyard
12. Butler Winery
13. Brown County Winery
14. Chateau Thomas Tasting Room
15. Simmons Winery
16. Shadey Lake Winery

SOUTHERN INDIANA
17. French Lick Winery
18. Huber Orchard and Winery
19. Turtle Run Winery and Orchard
20. Winzerwald Winery and Vineyard
21. Kauffman Winery

SOUTHERN INDIANA-EAST
22. Lanthier Winery and Tasting Room
23. The Thomas Family Winery
24. Madison Vineyards
25. Villa Milan Winery
26. Chateau Pomije Winery and Restaurant
27. The Ridge Winery

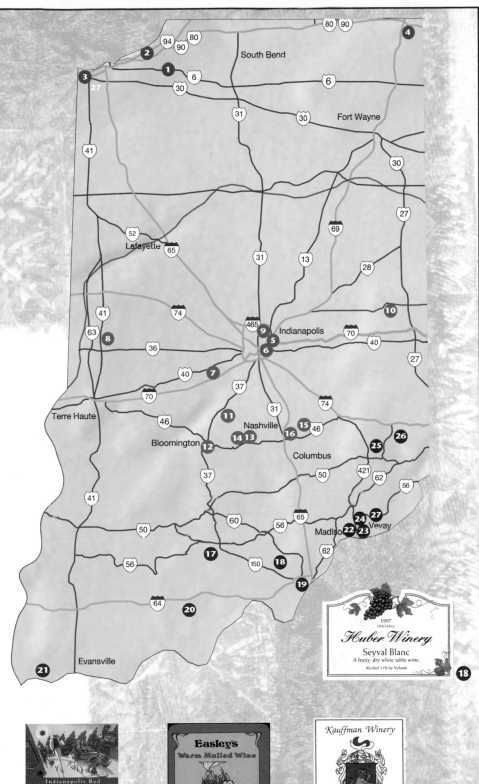

South Bend

Fort Wayne

Lafayette

Terre Haute

Indianapolis

Nashville

Bloomington

Columbus

Madison

Vevay

Evansville

1997
INDIANA
Huber Winery
Seyval Blanc
A fruity, dry white table wine.
Alcohol 11% by Volume

18

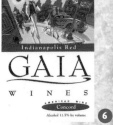

Indianapolis Red
GAIA
W I N E S
AMERICAN WINE
Concord
Alcohol 11.5% by volume

6

Easley's
Warm Mulled Wine

A LIGHT TABLE WINE WITH SPICES, HONEY,
FERMENTED CIDER, AND LEMON JUICE ADDED.

ALCOHOL 9% BY VOLUME

TO BE SERVED WARM, DO NOT BOIL.

Made and Bottled By
Easley Enterprises Inc.
Indianapolis, In B.W-IN-5

5

Kauffman Winery

Posey White
POSEY COUNTY, INDIANA

FINE SWEET TABLE WINE

PRODUCED AND BOTTLED BY
KAUFFMAN WINERY, MT. VERNON, INDIANA

CONTAINS SULFITES

21

Wineries of Indiana

A Guide to the Wineries
and Vineyards in Indiana

By D. L. Tadevich

PUBLISHING–PLUS

Publishing Plus:
A division of Insurance Publishing Plus Corporation
11690 Technology Drive
Carmel IN 46032 USA

Acknowledgements

I would like to thank all of those who participated in helping to create this guide. My special thanks go to Walter J. Gdowski, chairman and CEO of Insurance Publishing Plus, without whom this book would not have been published. I would also like to thank Dr. Charlie Thomas, Sally Linton, Jill Ditmire, and Jim Butler for their valuable input. Moreover, this guide would not have been possible to complete without the

help and encouragement of the Indiana Wine Grape Council. And finally, a special acknowledgment goes to Cheryl Rogers for allowing the use of her grape drawings, and my two daughters, Isabella and Melanie, who were my greatest and most enthusiastic supporters.

Wineries of Indiana

A Guide to the Wineries and Vineyards in Indiana

By D. L. Tadevich

Writer

D. L. Tadevich

Project Editor

Heidi Newman, Mark My Word!
proof@indy.net

Editors

Georgianna Quinn, Alice Roettger

Designer

Karen J. Kennedy, Major Productions, Inc.
major@clarityonline.com

Photographers

Jeff Robbins, Patricia Delaplane, Karen Kennedy

Special thanks to the Indiana Wine Grape Council for the use of their photographs

Grape Prints, Cheryl Rogers

First Edition, 2001

PUBLISHING–PLUS

Publishing Plus:
A division of Insurance Publishing Plus Corporation
11690 Technology Drive
Carmel IN 46032 USA
800-211-3257

ISBN 0-9704154-0-0

Printed in China

Distributed by
Partners Book Distributing Inc.
2325 Jarco Drive
Holt, MI 48842

Table of Contents

Introduction

The idea for this book came to me at Publishing Plus after I decided to go on a wine-tasting trek. I knew that there were a few wineries in Indiana and I could name at least two, but that was it. While attending the Indiana Wine Festival and learning that there were 23 wineries in the state–with more opening up–I decided that it was time for an Indiana wine travel book so that everyone could learn about, visit and enjoy Indiana's contributions to the wine industry.

Each winery projects its own image, reflecting its owner and/or winemaker. Some of the wineries grow their own grapes, while some buy them from around the United States, but each winery produces and bottles the wine at its own establishment. The wineries are open for wine tasting and sales on Sunday, as well as other days of the week. Children are welcome at the wineries, and there is always something for them to eat and drink, so take them along. The wineries also have gift shops of many varieties. They offer wine accessories and other things that are unique to the winery. Some of the gift shops sell cheeses, fruits and crackers to have with your wine, while other wineries provide these things for free if you are sampling their wines. One very special service that most of the wineries provide is personalizing wine labels. The customer can pick the greeting, type of wine and sometimes even a photo from their personal albums. All of these things will be printed on a label to add a personal touch to a memorable occasion. All wineries will accept telephone and fax orders and will ship wine to you. The bottles of wine range from $8.95 - $16.95. The berry wines are usually $12.95. Almost all of the wineries offer discounted prices for bulk orders. If you want to tour a specific winery, it is wise to call before you go to check the times and days of tours and to see if you need reservations.

Villa Milan Vineyard

Learning about wine can be an enjoyable experience on many levels. Since Indiana wines have many different styles and broad ranges to choose from, you will probably find a favorite that you will enjoy for years to come.

After years of cultivating French-American hybrids and native American grapes, Indiana winemakers are also growing the classic European Vitis vinifera grapes — these winemakers are considered to be bold since they are venturing into uncharted territory. The Indiana estates are planting Cabernets, Merlots and Pinot Noirs. The Midwest has harsh winters and a short growing season that can make grape growing difficult at best. Indiana winemakers are open to new blending techniques, thanks to more sophisticated winemaking processes and state-of-the-art equipment. Indiana wines have become very impressive, and can now compete with the best from California and around the world.

There are several wineries that are considered to be the pioneers of the Indiana wine industry: Oliver Winery, Easley Winery, Chateau Thomas Winery, Butler Winery, Huber Winery and Kauffman Winery. These wineries began in the 1970s and are responsible for changing wine laws in Indiana–and also for promoting the popularity of wine grape growing in our Hoosier State. They have come a long way with their knowledge of grape growing.

This book is organized into four sections: Central Indiana, South Central Indiana, Southern Indiana, and Northern Indiana. All Indiana wineries are within a two-hour drive from the capital, Indianapolis. The greatest number of wineries and vineyards are located in Southern Indiana (along the Ohio River) and to reach all of them in one trip, you will need at least a three-day weekend. There are five wineries in Central Indiana and four in the north.

I had a wonderful experience visiting the wineries, tasting their wines and talking to the winemakers. I hope that you will have a pleasant journey experiencing Indiana wines as well.

Please note that this book is not to educate anyone about wines or how to make wines. My section on How to Make Wine is a very brief synopsis on winemaking. If you would like to have more knowledge on how to make wines, ask any of the winemakers at the wineries or buy a book on winemaking. This is a book about traveling to, and the general history of, the wineries.

Cheers! 🍷

Indiana Wine Grape Council

By Sally Linton, Marketing Director
www.indianawines.org

Welcome to Indiana's wine industry, a place where the age-old art of winemaking becomes an ever-evolving craft, thanks to our unique Hoosier style.

As of this writing, Indiana is home to 23 wineries. That number may seem surprising to some, but Indiana has a rich grape-growing/wine-producing history. In fact, in the early 1800s, Indiana was the 10th largest grape producing state in the country. Prohibition put the Indiana wine industry on hold–and it took passage of the Small Winery Act in the early 1970s to once again allow wineries to sell directly to the public.

It didn't take long for the Indiana wine industry to bounce back, and because of the renewed interest in the trade, the Indiana Wine Grape Council was formed in 1989 to enhance the economic development of the wine and grape industry. Currently based at Purdue University, the Council provides support in enology, viticulture and marketing to new and existing wineries in Indiana.

Sales of over 180,000 gallons a year (that translates to about 900,000 bottles!) attest to the enjoyment of Indiana wines. Virtually every Indiana winery offers at least one award-winning wine, and most Indiana winemakers bring home medals from wine competitions throughout the nation. These awards include over 140 medals at the 2000 Indiana State Fair 'Indy International' wine competition, the third largest wine competition in the country.

Indiana wine tours make a great choice for a day trip or weekend excursion with companions. Each winery offers its own atmosphere and signature style of wine, yet all 23 share one important quality–passion for the product. To discover many of the Indiana wineries in one location, join us for the Vintage Indiana Wine & Food Festival, held each June in Indianapolis. 🍷

A Brief Synopsis of Indiana's Wine History

By Jim Butler, Butler Winery

European settlers tried for over two hundred years to establish vineyards in Eastern North America without success. It wasn't until a group of French speaking Swiss immigrants settled in Indiana that this long-sought goal was achieved.

The leader of the group, John James Dufour, arrived in America in 1796, looking for land to settle a colony of "vinedressers" where they could grow grapes and make wine. He had only gold and silver watches that he had brought from Switzerland to use as money. He found a group of prosperous merchants west of the Appalachian Mountains in Lexington, Kentucky, who were willing to finance a vineyard. In 1799, Dufour planted vines that he had purchased in Baltimore and Philadelphia that were advertised to be of European stock. Unfortunately, in the summer of 1802, all but two of the 21 varieties had begun to fail. Only the Cape and Madeira vines, which were actually not pure European varieties, survived. This lack of success caused the investors to lose interest in the project.

The winemaking colony, with the help of Thomas Jefferson, received a 2,500-acre land grant in the Indiana territory on the north bank of the Ohio River. They founded a town they called Vevay. It was here that the Swiss vine growers successfully grew the Cape and Madeira grapes and consequently, America's first commercial wines were produced.

Of the two varieties, the Cape was the more important. It was a late-ripening, thick-skinned grape that made wine described variously as "of an inferior quality" to "superior to the common Bordeaux." The wine was sold to markets as far away as Cincinnati, Louisville, Lexington and St. Louis.

Dufour decided to go back to Europe in order to get more supplies. Unfortunately, he was captured while at sea and was unable to return for 10 years. Still, the Swiss vinedressers kept the vineyards going. By the time Dufour returned, they had well over 40 acres of grapes near Vevay, in what we now refer to as Switzerland County.

In 1819, articles and letters in American agricultural magazines regarded Vevay, Indiana, as the most promising wine growing venture in the country. Still, continued success and expansion were struck down by events beyond their control. It was discovered that corn was easily made into whiskey and whiskey was easily made into money. The wine industry was slowly dying because of this new liquor profit. Then, an economic depression that began about 1819 hit the frontier terribly hard.

By the mid 1820s, the vineyards were in serious decline. The original settlers were getting older. The generation coming of age found more profit in growing corn and potatoes. When new grape varieties appeared in the mid-1820s, the residents of Vevay, Indiana, were financially unable to replant their vineyards.

In 1826, a year before his death, John James Dufour published *The American Vinedresser's Guide*. It was the first book written about American grape growing and winemaking. It stood as the best reference for many years.

Cincinnati was the wine capital of the country from the 1840s through the 1860s. The success of the Cincinnati industry was based upon the Catawba grape. Vineyards extended down the Ohio River from Cincinnati to Georgetown, Indiana. Even after the collapse of the Cincinnati industry around 1870, wineries were found scattered across Southern Indiana until the beginning of prohibition in 1919.

American grape diseases found their way to Europe in the mid-1860s, with devastating results. The French proceeded to cross their vines with North American stock to produce varieties with more disease resistance. In the mid-1960s, these new French varieties formed the basis for the planting of new vineyards in Indiana. The Indiana laws governing wineries started becoming more liberal in 1971. Today, twenty-three wineries are found in the state and several more are in the planning stages. These wineries range from small, traditional cellars, to large, modern production facilities. Two hundred years of history and tradition are coming to fruition. 🍷

Food and Wine Pairing

By Jill A. Ditmire

We all have our favorite foods and wines, and the number one rule for enjoying either is to create your own palate. There are no rules when it comes to pairing food and wine, simply guidelines. However, if you like steak with Chardonnay, then eat steak with Chardonnay. If someone tells you that it's wrong, then don't have dinner with them. If you want to take your enjoyment of food and wine to another level, there are generally two ways to go about pairing the two–complementary and contrast pairing.

Complementary pairing means selecting dishes and wines that have similar qualities–be it taste, structure or style. Rich, creamy foods are best served with rich, creamy wines. Wines aged in oak go well with buttery or smoked foods. Tart, young wines with a hint of spice are perfect for highly seasoned cuisine.

Contrast pairing is just like it sounds–pick a food and wine combination that offers the mouth two opposite tastes. Rich, creamy foods contrast nicely with crisp, tart wines. Sweet, fruity wines add an unusual twist to hot, spicy foods. These guidelines hold true for both red and white wines, and by following them, one gets away from the old "red wine is for meat, white wine is for fish" dilemma.

Indiana wines make terrific food partners. You simply have to try the different varietals and decide which ones suit your taste buds the best. You will find familiar wine varietals grown in Indiana (Cabernet Sauvignon, Cabernet Franc, Riesling), but I urge you to give some of the others a try. Both native American and French-American hybrid grapes flourish in Hoosier soils, creating some delicious and affordable alternatives to an expensive bottle of wine produced somewhere else in the world.

The Whites

Chardonel is made by many Indiana wineries. Usually it spends a bit of time in oak barrels, creating a medium-bodied wine with pear aromas, hints of butterscotch and tropical fruit. One of its parents is the Chardonnay grape, so enjoy Chardonel with foods you might normally pair with Chardonnay, like creamy white pasta sauces, Middle Eastern fare (baba ganoush, hummus, moussaka), smoked, sautéed or grilled fish, lobster, roast chicken, chicken piccata and pork. It also makes the perfect white wine for your Thanksgiving turkey, whether it is smoked, deep-fried or oven roasted.

Ditmire is the creator, producer and host of "The Good Life with Jill Ditmire." This is a weekly PBS television show which explores, educates and entertains viewers about wines and foods that are not only from the Midwest, but also from around the world. Jill also contributes regular features on food and wine to Indianapolis Monthly, DINE *magazine and* Indywine.com.

Seyval Blanc can be made in a number of different styles, bringing out different characteristics of the grape. Most wineries produce a medium-bodied style that has hints of melon, pear and tropical fruit. It's wonderful when enjoyed with cheese (Brie, Gouda, Swiss, Fontina), seafood (scallops, shrimp, oysters, grilled lobster), Indian cuisine (green and red curries, saag paneer, biryani of all types, tandoori chicken), red or white sauce pasta dishes and, of course, is great when sipped on its own.

Vidal Blanc is usually made in the style of a grassy, tart Sauvignon Blanc, making it an excellent food partner. Try Vidal in place of Sauvignon Blanc with pasta (white clam sauce, pasta primavera, spicy red sauce), Thai food (Pad Thai, satay, tom kha gai soup), fish (sautéed dover sole, grilled halibut, orange roughy), chicken and pork. It also goes well with vegetable-based dishes like roasted eggplant, Chinese stir-fry dishes and lentil soup.

Vignoles can be blended to produce a sweet, semi-dry wine exhibiting aromas of peach and apricot with a touch of sweetness. This is another great sipping wine; it is very light and fruity. Pair it with appetizers like mild cheeses (Havarti, Port Salut), sour cream- or cream cheese-based dips with crackers or vegetables, salsas (the sweetness of the wine takes the bite out of a spicy pepper), Cajun cuisine, sushi Maki rolls or with fresh fruit for dessert.

Often, the three (Seyval Blanc, Vidal Blanc and Vignoles) are combined to produce a wonderful food wine that resembles a Riesling. This blend is another great appetizer wine, pairing well with all of the Vignoles-friendly foods mentioned above.

Cayuga is a native American grape that makes a crisp, slightly sweet white wine. It's just right for sipping before dinner or served with light fare such as cold pasta salads, tuna salad sandwiches or poached chicken.

Catawba is also a native American grape that produces a light, white wine with a floral nose and a fruity, almost White Zinfandel-like taste. Enjoy Catawba with fresh fruit or mild cheeses like Monterrey Jack, Colby and Baby Swiss.

Niagara is yet another native American grape and is widely produced in Indiana. Bottled on its own or blended with other grapes, the taste is just like eating fresh, cold, white grapes. It makes the perfect patio or picnic sipper.

The Reds

Chambourcin grapes make a spicy wine with flavors of blackberry and currants with enough tannin to be enjoyed in place of Cabernet Sauvignon with a meal. It's especially nice with game–like roasted venison, pheasant, steak, prime rib and hearty, beef-based stews.

Chancellor produces a berry-nosed red wine that often imitates a soft Pinot Noir with fruit aromas and soft tannins. Chancellor goes great with meaty pasta sauces and Italian cuisine such as lasagna, bolognese, manicotti and chicken parmigiana. It also pairs nicely with beef tenderloin, lamb chops, roast duck, baked salmon and grilled tuna steaks. Chancellor is a good red wine choice for your Thanksgiving dinner.

The Concord is a native American grape that most people have tried without the alcohol–it's the grape used in Welch's Grape Juice. If you like sweet wines, this one goes great with pizza, chili con carne, beef tacos, macaroni and cheese and hot dogs on the grill.

Indiana fruit wines can make a memorable meal. Dry-style blueberry and cherry wines are excellent partners for duck, pork and salmon. Serve them cool to room temperature–not chilled–to bring out the fruit taste. A sweeter, fruit wine like peach, strawberry or blackberry makes a wonderful dessert on its own. Set a bottle in the refrigerator to enjoy after a meal. Better yet, slowly simmer the wine in a saucepan until it reduces and thickens. The natural fruit pectin creates a syrupy, rich sauce that is heavenly over cheesecake, pound cake, fresh berries or ice cream.

Of course, the ultimate food wine is sparkling wine or Champagne. These two are essentially the same, but you can only call it Champagne (with a capital C) if it comes from the Champagne region of France. Several Indiana wineries produce some delicious sparklers–Anderson's Orchard and Winery, Huber Winery, Gaia Wines and Easley Winery–just to name a few. Each makes a distinctly different style of sparkling wine suitable with an appetizer, main course or dessert. When you don't know what wine to serve with a meal, choose a sparkler. Both your guests and your menu will thank you. ☙

Recipes

By Jill A. Ditmire

Chicken Piccata
serve with Indiana Chardonel

Serves 8

2 pounds	boneless, skinless chicken breasts
1/3 cup	all-purpose flour
	Kosher salt
	Cayenne pepper
	Freshly ground black pepper
1/3 cup	olive oil
2 T	butter
1 cup	water
1/2 cup	Chardonel wine
2	medium-sized lemons
	lemon thyme

With a meat mallet, pound chicken breasts to 1/8-inch thick cutlets. Do this by placing meat between wax paper and pounding until thin. Sprinkle with salt and ground peppers. Next, lightly sprinkle each cutlet with flour, coating all of the meat. In a 12-inch skillet over medium-high heat, add olive oil and butter until melted. Cook each chicken cutlet until golden brown on each side (you may need more oil–add as needed, but use a light hand). When browned, remove cutlets from pan.

Reduce heat to low and deglaze pan with water and wine, scraping the bottom and incorporating any drippings from cutlets. Add a pinch of salt, then return chicken to pan. Cover and simmer for 15 minutes until cutlets are fork-tender. Do not overcook!

Cut lemons in half. Squeeze the juice of 1/2 lemon onto cutlets, remove from pan and transfer to serving plate. Cover to keep warm. Squeeze remaining lemons into pan liquid, stirring constantly. Bring to a boil over high heat.

Remove from heat and spoon liquid over chicken cutlets. Sprinkle with freshly chopped lemon thyme or dried thyme and serve immediately.

This Chicken Piccata is the perfect match for Indiana Chardonel. The medium-bodied wine offers aromas of tropical fruits, which enhance the lemony tartness of the dish. Chardonel that spent time in oak also delivers a buttery richness which complements the tasty sauce.

Veal and Mushroom Pasta
also works well as Venison and Mushroom Pasta

Serves 4

This is an Italian-inspired, earthy dish that brings out the best in an Indiana Chambourcin wine.

1 cup	*canned, imported Italian plum tomatoes, cut and drained of juice*
3 T	*butter*
1 T	*olive oil*
1/4 cup	*chopped onion*
3.5 ounces	*(1 package) of shiitake mushrooms, stems discarded and tops diced*
1/2 Pound	*Veal (or Ground Venison)*
	Kosher salt
	Freshly ground black pepper
1/4 cup	*Pecorino Romano Cheese, freshly grated*
	Cooked pasta — choose one which will let the sauce cling to it. If your family desires tubes, try penne; if strands, choose fettucine.

In a small saucepan over medium heat, add butter and oil. Cook onion, stirring often until pale gold in color. Add the veal and stir until browned all over. Next, add mushrooms, tomatoes and generous pinches of salt and pepper. Don't be salt-shy, mushrooms need it and it brings out the flavor in the veal. Your sauce will have no flavor without it. Cook at a steady, but gentle, simmer for 15 to 20 minutes.

When ready to serve, add pasta to sauce, swirl in 1 Tablespoon of butter and Pecorino Romano cheese.

ENJOY!!

This simple, yet bold-flavored dish brings out the earthy, berry qualities of an Indiana Chambourcin. The peppers and mushrooms love the similar truffle-like qualities of Chambourcin, while the tannins of the wine balance the rich buttery veal sauce and marry well with the slight acid from the tomatoes in the sauce. Using venison instead of veal in the dish only adds more depth of flavor–which creates even more delight both in the dish and in the glass.

How Wine Is Made

This section is intended to be a very brief overview.

Winemaking

The winemaker is the person who turns grapes into wine. *Enology* is the science of wines and winemaking. An enologist has earned a degree in the science of winemaking. *Viticulture* is the science, or art, of grape growing. *Vinification* is the process of turning grape juice into wine.

Grape Harvest

Harvest time can vary, but it usually lasts from late August through September—or even into October. Harvest is a winery's busiest season, and those wineries that cultivate their own grapes usually work around the clock. In Indiana, the grapes are picked by hand. This is done in a very gingerly fashion, in order not to break the skins of the grapes. (Air causes oxidation in the grapes, which gives the wine a vinegar taste.) The grapes are then transported to the winery.

Red Wine

The red grapes are not harvested until they are as ripe as possible. The fruit's ripeness is an important factor in the quality of the red wine. It is the skin of the red-wine grapes that gives the wine its color, tannin and the many fruit flavors that red wine lovers enjoy. Once the grapes have been picked, the under-ripe and rotten ones are discarded. The grapes are then lightly crushed into a thick mush, called "must," and all stalks are removed. The must is then transferred into stainless steel tanks or oak barrels for fermentation. The grapes sit in their juices and soften for at least a couple of days before the winemaker begins the fermentation process.

Using cultured yeast for fermentation, the winemaker sets the temperature in the tanks at 77-86 degrees Fahrenheit. The temperature must remain constant throughout the fermentation process. When all of the sugar has turned into alcohol, fermentation has taken place. This usually takes about three to four weeks.

The drier wines will usually go through a second fermentation, called malolactic, or just malo, in which the wine is left to sit on the skins for one to four weeks after the first fermentation. During this time, the color will redden and the tannin will soften. (Tannin is in the skin of the red grape and gives a dry taste to the wine. You can usually taste tannin if you bite into a red grape seed.)

Finally, the juice is drawn from the tank. The first juice is called the free-run, because it freely runs out of the tank. The remaining juice, with its excessive tannin, is squeezed out by a winepress. It is then mixed in with the free-run juice (in proportions chosen by the individual winemaker) in order to adjust the tannin level in the wine. The wine is clarified to rid it of solids and remove any cloudiness. Sulfur dioxide is then added to protect against bacteria before bottling. Finally, the wine is placed in stainless steel tanks or oak barrels to age. When it reaches the determined maturation date, the wine is bottled.

How long should wine age? Some wine is sold immediately to the consumer. If the winery is producing a fine wine, it could sit for one year or more before distribution.

White Wine

It is trickier for the winemaker to make a good white wine than to make a good red wine. The white grape skins are thin and, consequently, can rot faster or overcook in the sun. Because the fruit must be harvested at just the right time, it becomes a delicate balancing act between too soon and too late.

White grapes go to the pressing machines, where the skins are gently split open, and the grape juice is immediately separated from the skins and stems. (For a drier white, the juice is left in contact with the skins for a longer time.) The wine is now ready for fermentation. As with the red grapes, fermentation takes place when the winemaker adds cultured yeast, however white grapes are fermented at a cooler temperature–41-86 degrees Fahrenheit.

Fermentation can take weeks or months. The lower temperatures create a light, crisp wine. Yet, the warmer the temperature, the fuller the wine. The aging process takes place either in oak barrels or stainless steel tanks. For a fruitier wine, the entire process of filtering, fermenting and bottling can take only a few months before the wine goes to the customer. For finer wines, the maturing process can take a year or longer.

Rosé–or a more modern name–Blush Wine

Blush wines are made from red grapes, but with the same processing as white wines. The juice is allowed a very short period of contact, usually a few hours, with the skins before they're removed–giving blush its "pink" color. Consequently, very little tannin is absorbed from the skins and

therefore, the blush wine can be chilled like a white wine. Because of the tannin in the skin of red grapes, red wine should not be chilled; if so, it can taste bitter.

Blending the grapes

Many wines–both red and white–are blends of different grape varieties. Different wines can be fermented separately and then brought together later. The winemaker can blend different barrels of wine from the same grape variety, or wines from different vineyards, or even different regions, to create one kind of wine before bottling. Blending grapes is an age-old tradition in the United States, Europe and just about anywhere that you can find a winemaker.

It is a misconception that wine, red or white, aged in oak is better than wine aged in stainless steel. There really isn't any correlation between wine quality and the use of oak–it is a matter of individual taste. Many people love to argue this matter, but it is entirely up to the wine drinker's palate.

Tastes most associated with oak aging are nutmeg, vanilla, chocolate or smoke. There are some distinctions between different types of oak. American oak imparts vanilla and coconut flavors to the wines, while French oak imparts a more subtle taste.

Sparkling Wines

Almost all sparkling wine is made from white wine. The winemaking production method begins the same as with still wine–the grapes are pressed quickly and then fermented to create a dry wine. Most of the wines made for sparkling wine are fermented in stainless steel tanks.

The two methods that are frequently used to make sparkling wines are the Methode Champenoise, a traditional method of second fermentation in the bottle, and the Charmat method in which carbon dioxide gas is trapped in the tank and fermentation takes place there.

When grape juice ferments, carbon dioxide gas is released into the atmosphere. However, if the winemaker wants to produce sparkling wine, the carbon dioxide gas must be prevented from escaping.

If the winemaker is using the Champenoise method to make the sparking wine, the wine stays in the same bottle from the second fermentation until it is sold. During the bottling process, a mixture of yeast and sugar is added before the bottle is capped or corked and secured with a metal clasp, called a graffe. The bottles of wine are

stored on their sides in an environment with a cool, consistent temperature.

The second fermentation takes place in the bottle when all of the sugar turns to alcohol (three-four weeks). The bottles are left untouched for at least 12 months–or up to three years, for the higher quality sparkling wines. During this time, a slow a process called autolysis takes place. The spent yeast cells come in contact with the wine in the bottle and are slowly destroyed by their own enzymes. The autolysis process is important to the taste factor. The longer the yeast is in contact with the wine, the more the flavor takes on the yeast characteristics.

There are still sediments left in the wine, so winemakers use a method called riddling, a gentle turning of the bottles by hand, to get the sediments to settle onto the cap and eventually pop out. The neck of the bottle is submerged in a solution with temperatures below freezing. The idea is to freeze the sediment resting upon the cap into an ice plug. Once frozen, the winemaker turns the bottle up and pops off the cap. The sediment, trapped in its ice cube, shoots out of the bottle. The bottle is then resealed with the champagne cork.

The entire Champenoise method usually takes anywhere from 18-40 months. This method is very labor intensive and is reserved for the higher quality grape varieties.

Another important factor is the length of time the sparkling wine sits in storage. In the second fermentation, the carbon dioxide is trapped. The longer the wine sits, the more the gas becomes incorporated into the wine, and the more slowly it is released from the wine in the glass.

The Charmat method of making sparkling wine, which is much faster and less labor intensive, is also less expensive. The still wine is transferred to a closed, pressurized tank to capture the carbon dioxide, and sugar and yeast are added to it to create a sparkling wine. The wine is then filtered, clarified and finally, bottled.

GLOSSARY OF WINE TERMS

By Dr. Charles Thomas, The Chateau Thomas Winery

Acidic A wine that is unbalanced; tending to have too much acid–making it sharp, sour, tart or acrid.

Aftertaste (or Finish) The lingering impression of the taste of the wine after swallowing. It may be short, average, lingering or long (a lingering finish is usually indicative of a quality wine).

Aroma The scents or odors that originate from the grape and soil. Aromas are present in young wines and tend to disappear with extended aging.

Balance Refers to the proportion or harmony of the various elements of wine taste such as acid, sweetness and tannins.

Barrel-fermented Refers to the fermentation of wine in small oak barrels rather than in a tank. (See Sur-Lie)

Bland A wine that has little character or taste; generally low in acid and tannin;, vapid, insipid.

Body The tactile impression of fullness on the palate due to alcohol, glycerin and residual sugar.

Bouquet The scents or odors that originate from the winemaking process such as barrel aging, malolactic fermentation and bottle aging. Bouquet emerges as the wine matures.

Complex(ity) A wine containing many different aromas, bouquets and flavors producing a pleasing harmony.

Corky (Corked) A wine that has a musty, dank or dead mouse smell. This smell is usually caused by an infected cork and should be discarded.

Dry A wine that contains no sugar; the absence of sweetness.

Earthy A wine that smells like freshly turned soil, an aroma that usually adds to the pleasant complexity of the wine.

Extract The non-sugar wine solids dissolved in alcohol, which contribute to its weight and body.

Fermentation The process of converting sugars to ethyl alcohol by yeasts added to the the juice of fruits or vegetables. Carbon dioxide and water are by-products of this process. (See Malolactic Fermentation)

Filtered A wine clarified by use of a filter to remove yeasts, bacteria and other solids that can detract from the wine quality after bottling.

Fining A clarifying technique that introduces an electrolytic agent such as egg whites, gelatin, bentonite clay or one of many other agents to instantly bond with unwanted solids in the wine. These will settle to the bottom of the tank before the clean wine is removed (racking) and do not remain a part of the finished product.

Fortified A wine to which alcohol has been added to increase its alcoholic strength, usually to 15-21%.

Foxy The strong smell of native American grape species (Vitis labrusca), which has the musky smell of a caged animal.

Fruity The fragrance or flavor of usually young wines which is reminiscent of grapes or other fruits.

Full-Bodied The feel in the mouth when a wine is high in alcohol and/or extract.

Grassy Green, floral aromas, like freshly mown hay, cut grass, etc.

Herbaceous Smelling like or reminiscent of herbs.

Lees The sediment that accumulates after clarification or fermentation in a tank or barrel. It usually consists of dead yeast cells and proteins.

Legs The "tears", or streams, of wine which cling to the sides of the glass after swirling. This is caused by differential evaporation of alcohol and other liquids in the wine. Legs generally indicate higher alcoholic content and body.

Maderized A color and flavor change due to extended aging of a wine. Consists of brownish coloration and loss of fruit flavors with development of varying degrees of caramel, or even shoe polish, odors.

Malolactic Fermentation A secondary fermentation caused by bacteria which ferments malic acid (a sharp acid) to lactic acid (a softer acid). This is done to soften a wine's acidity and also produces "buttery" bouquets.

Methode Champenoise The traditional method of producing sparkling wine by causing a secondary fermentation in the bottle instead of a tank. This produces the highest quality sparkling wines.

Nutty Aromas or bouquets reminiscent of nuts.

Off-Dry A wine that is slightly sweet or almost dry.

Oxidized Bouquets in old or oxygen-exposed wine like sherry, caramel, nuts and shoe polish.

Racking The process of drawing off, or siphoning off, clean wine to separate it from sediment or the lees in a barrel or tank.

Residual sugar The unfermented or added sugars in a wine at bottling, usually expressed as percent/100 ml.

Rich The full flavors of a wine.

Robust The character of a full-bodied, full-flavored wine which is heavy and tannic.

Round A wine that is smooth and gentle due to a particular alcohol/acid/tannin balance which makes the wine feel "round" in the mouth.

Sediment Deposits precipitated in the bottle of an aged wine.

Semi-Dry Similar to off-dry.

Semi-Sweet A wine that is slightly, or somewhat, sweet.

Spicy A wine with aromas and flavors which evoke an impression of spice.

Sweet A wine that contains sugar in sufficient quantities to be perceptively sweet (1% residual sugar), or definitely sweet at more than 2% residual sugar.

Sur-Lie Refers to leaving the newly fermented wine in the barrel with the lees of fermentation in order to create more body and complexity.

Tannic A wine that is unbalanced, tending to have too much tannin, making it bitter or astringent on the finish. Usually a young, barrel-aged wine.

Tannin An astringent acid derived from the skins, seeds and wooden barrels which causes a puckery sensation in the mouth and throat. It is an essential preservative for quality wines.

Unbalanced A wine lacking harmony in its acid, sugar, and tannin components, usually with one dominating the others.

Varietal Refers to a wine named after the grape variety from which it was made or to a wine made entirely from a single grape variety.

Vegetal Any odor of vegetables or leafy substances such as asparagus or green beans.

Viticultural Area (Appellation) A delimited region where common geographical or climatic qualities contribute to a definable character of a wine. In the U.S., they are generally defined by geography alone.

Vitis labrusca A species of grapes native to North America, including Concord, Catawba and Niagara, which are winter-hardy and used to produce wine, jellies, and jam.

Vitis riparia One of the North American species of grapes.

Vitis vinifera Species of European grapes; Vitis vinifera, known as "the wine bearers," are the "old world grapes" used to make the finest wines in the world, such as Chardonnay, Cabernet Sauvignon, and Pinot Noir.

Wine The product of the fermentation of grapes and other fruits or vegetables.

Grape Varietal Types

Aurora A light-bodied, white French-American hybrid grape

Blaufrankisch A full-bodied, aromatic, red vinifera grape

Cabernet Franc A full-bodied, aromatic, red vinifera grape

Cabernet Sauvignon A full-bodied, aromatic, red vinifera grape

Catawba A deep-pink-skinned, fruity, American hybrid grape

Chambourcin A full-bodied, aromatic, red French-American hybrid grape

Chancellor A full-bodied, aromatic, red French-American hybrid grape

Chardonel A full-bodied, white French-American hybrid grape

Carignane A full-bodied, aromatic, red vinifera hybrid grape

Carnelian A full-bodied, aromatic, red vinifera hybrid grape

Chardonnay A tropical, full-bodied, white vinifera grape

Chenin Blanc A light-bodied, fruity, white vinifera grape

Concord A full-bodied, aromatic, red native American grape

De Chaunac A full-bodied, aromatic, red French-American hybrid grape

Gewurztraminer A light-bodied, spicy, white vinifera grape

Grenache A medium-bodied, aromatic, red vinifera grape

Leon Millot A full-bodied, aromatic, red French-American hybrid grape

Marechal Foch A full-bodied, aromatic, red French-Riparia hybrid grape

Merlot A full-bodied, aromatic, red vinifera grape

Muscat A light-bodied, floral, white vinifera grape

Muscat Canelli A light-bodied, floral, white vinifera grape

Niagara A medium-bodied, white French-American hybrid grape

Petit Sirah A full-bodied, aromatic, red vinifera grape

Pinot Noir A medium-bodied, aromatic, red vinifera grape

Ravat 51 A full-bodied, aromatic, white French-American hybrid grape

Riesling A light-bodied, floral, white vinifera grape

Sangiovese A medium-bodied, aromatic, red vinifera grape

Sauvignon Blanc An herbal, full-bodied, white vinifera grape

Seibel 13053 A full-bodied, aromatic, red French-American hybrid grape

Seyval Blanc A medium-bodied, white French-American hybrid grape

Steuben A pink-skinned, fruity, French-American hybrid grape

Syrah A full-bodied, aromatic, red vinifera grape

Vidal Blanc A medium-bodied, white French-American hybrid grape

Vignoles A medium-bodied, white French-American hybrid grape

Zinfandel A full-bodied, aromatic, red vinifera grape

How to Read a Wine Label

1997
Vintage year.

Estate Bottled
All grapes were
grown, fermented,
blended and bottled
from this vineyard.

Creekbend Vineyard
All of the grapes are
from this vineyard.

Cabernet Sauvignon
Grape variety. The
wine must contain a
minimum of 75%
Cabernet Sauvignon
grapes.

Alcohol by Volume
Actual alcohol content.

OLIVER
*While most woodpeckers are seen in
wooded areas, the Red Headed Woodpecker
prefers the open fields of southern Indiana.
This beautiful bird can often be seen
swooping low across a country road after
flying insects.*
*Our Mission at Oliver Winery is to produce
world class wines that emphasize varietal
character and complexity. For more information, or to order wine, call us toll free at
the number below.*

PRODUCED &
BOTTLED BY
OLIVER WINERY
BLOOMINGTON, IN
(812) 876-5800
(800) 258-2783
CONTAINS SULFITES
FOR SALE IN
INDIANA ONLY

GOVERNMENT WARNING: (1) ACCORDING TO THE
SURGEON GENERAL, WOMEN SHOULD NOT DRINK ALCOHOLIC
BEVERAGES DURING PREGNANCY BECAUSE OF THE RISK OF
BIRTH DEFECTS. (2) CONSUMPTION OF ALCOHOLIC BEVERAGES
IMPAIRS YOUR ABILITY TO DRIVE A CAR OR OPERATE MACHINERY,
AND MAY CAUSE HEALTH PROBLEMS.

Wines made in the United States whose labels
indicate that they contain a particular variety
of the grape must contain at least 75 percent
of that varietal. The other 25 percent can be a
less expensive grape. Most wines are blended
with grape varieties to give a particular taste.
Some premium wines are blends of several
varieties, or blends of grapes from the same
variety, with no one variety containing over 75
percent. These wines are labeled "table
wines". The U.S. wine industry created the
term "Meritage" for superior blended wines,
both red and white.

For Sale in Indiana Only
Grapes not grown in Indiana, or
grown in Indiana, but not in a
state-designated viticultural area.

The Art of Wine Tasting

Compliments of the Indiana Wine Grape Council

Visual

To really examine a wine, hold a glassful in the air against either light from a window, a white background, or a lamp. The color of the wine changes depending on the particular grape variety. Wines with deep color are usually fuller tasting. In a red wine, the purple color indicates a young wine and a red-brown indicates an older vintage. As for white wines, a young wine will be nearly colorless and an aged white wine will be a gold or deep gold color.

Smelling or Sniffing

Pour about one to two ounces of wine in your glass, hold it by the stem and swirl the wine to release the aromas. After you swirl, put your nose to the rim and deep into the glass, making the upper rim touch the bridge of your nose. You will smell fruity, spicy, or wood odors.

Swirl

Gently swirl the wine in the glass to release the aromas and let it air out before tasting it.

Tasting

When you are out wine tasting, it is better to taste the white wines before the red wines, dry before sweet wines, and older vintages before young wines. Swish a mouthful of wine around so it touches all sides of your tongue and the roof of your mouth. If you are sampling a dry red

wine, aerate it by imitating the motion of whistling backward to draw in air with the wine in your mouth. The air should change the taste in your mouth.

Spitting

If you are touring many wineries, it is advisable to spit–and don't be shy about it. Wineries do not take offense at this and often have a bucket for you to spit in. If you are shy about spitting, just take a sip and leave the rest. Then ask for just a taste of additional samples.

Storing

When storing wine, the cork must be kept moist. The bottle should be placed on its side or upside down. Wine should be kept in a room that is cool, 55-65 degrees Fahrenheit, and should not be exposed to heat or direct sunlight.

Serving

Before serving champagne or sparkling wine, it is good to chill it for three hours at 40 degrees Fahrenheit. White wines should chill for two hours at 45-50 degrees Fahrenheit. Red wine is served at room temperature, usually 60-65 degrees Fahrenheit and should be opened to air for one hour before serving. Air softens the tannins and intensifies the bouquet. 🍷

Wine Bottles

There is a difference between red and white wine bottles.

White Wine Bottle

Lead capsules were used until recently. Now, capsules must be made from plastic or tin foil.

The wine is usually below the bottom of the cork–there should be a small gap.

White wine bottles usually do not have the classic "shoulders," or shape of the red bottles.

Red Wine Bottle

Instead of a plastic capsule, a small seal at the top of the cork is used, giving a more contemporary look.

This is the classic Bordeaux shape with high shoulders. It is also used for many reds, such as Merlot and Zinfandel.

The glass most commonly used for bottles is either dark green or dark brown. The dark color provides protection against light and heat.

Sparkling Wine Bottle

The foil used is for decoration only and is supposed to add to the prestige of the sparkling wine.

Dark glass is always used with quality sparkling wines because light and heat easily damage them.

In the U.S., the words "sparkling wine" appear on the label. Outside of the U.S., the word Champagne is used to describe wine from that famous region of France. In the U.S., a winery can put the word champagne on the label, but not with a capital C.

Champagne Glass

The champagne glass is very narrow. This is to conserve the bubbles and to reveal all of the complex flavors.

Grapes from Indiana

Indiana has a short growing season and wine grape growers have to take this into consideration before selecting their grapes. Southern Indiana has the most vineyards because it is next to the Ohio

River, which gives off a cool breeze in the summer, while the hilly slopes in the region protect the vines against the harsh winter winds. This is also the only designated viticultural area in Indiana at the moment.

Native American

Native American grapes are hardy and plentiful in the East and Midwest. They can withstand the harsh winters and are resistant to diseases and insects. Early American grape growers did not know that American vines harbored a vine louse called phylloxera in their roots. American vines were resistant to the disease, but the European Vitis vinifera was not. American vines were transported to Europe in the 1880s, and phylloxera almost destroyed the European vines. French winemakers had to leave their homeland in order to find land that had not yet been poisoned by phylloxera. The French viticulturists began grafting French vines to American rootstocks. The results were French-American hybrids, which are premium grapes for winemaking. The American trunks were very resistant to phylloxera and the French vines were not harmed in any way when they were paired with the new trunks. Keeping the characteristics of the French grapes was a major concern since they had a very unique flavor. Both native American and French hybrids are grown commercially in Indiana, throughout the Midwest, in the Eastern United States and in parts of Europe. Unfortunately, like many other germs, the phylloxera strain has become too powerful, even for the American roots. Many California vines were destroyed in 1996 because of it. Still, there is always science to turn to and other vines to crossbreed.

Vinifera

The classic European wines come from Vitis vinifera grapes. These grapes grow best in a long growing season with warm days and cool nights, such as in France, Italy, Spain and California. In the U.S., most of the vinifera grapes are grown on the west coast in California, Oregon and Washington. However, many of the Eastern and Midwestern viticulturists are successfully cultivating these grapes with the vineyards that are near large bodies of water. These locations naturally protect vineyards against harsh winds, snows, and droughts.

A Varietal

A varietal wine is named after the grape or fruit that it is made from and must contain at least 75 percent of that one variety. ♀

These wineries are along Lake Michigan and are easy to incorporate into a weekend trip. The wineries in this section are Anderson Orchard and Winery, Dune Ridge Winery, Lake Michigan Winery and Satek Winery.

Anderson Vineyard

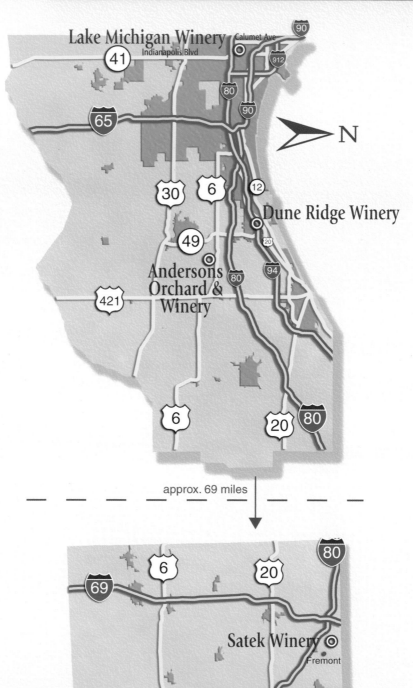

Lake Michigan Winery

Calumet Ave

Indianapolis Blvd

90

912

41

80

90

65

N

30

6

12

Dune Ridge Winery

49

20

Andersons
Orchard &
Winery

80

94

421

6

20

80

approx. 69 miles

6

20

80

69

Satek Winery

Fremont

Anderson Orchard and Winery

To get to Anderson Winery from Indianapolis, take I-65 North to I-80/94 East (Toll Road), follow this to IN-49 South and turn left on US-6 East, and go 3 miles. Watch for signs.

This winery takes on the sand dune look, while the northern terrain can be felt when first approaching the area. The interior of the winery is set up very much like a country store in which you want to touch everything. The fruit from the orchard looks succulent and is displayed well. The sculpture garden, with plenty of seating, is a new addition and is a great place to enjoy wine with friends and family. While you are there, take a tour around the premises. You'll find many treasures and plenty of fresh fruit hanging from the trees.

David Lundstom always dreamed of owning a winery. He thought it would be the best possible life that one could have. He started an agricultural operation in the 1980s with the intent of setting up a winery, but as David said, "It just wasn't a good time to start an agricultural business." Until 1993, David was an emergency medical services educator. Yet, owning a winery was never far from his mind, and he continued making wine in his basement and going to wine seminars. Bill Anderson

approached David about buying his orchard – David didn't need to think twice. This provided an excellent opportunity for him to build a winery and start a vineyard. In the fall of 1994, he opened the doors and sold the winery's first bottle of Orchard Blush. Today, he has planted 9.5 acres of grapevines, both viniferas and hybrids, and will soon start to offer estate wines.

David entered his sparkling wine made of Vidal and Seyval Blanc in the 2000 Indy International Wine Festival. Out of 66 competitors, his sparkling wine won the only gold medal! His Orchard Cherry also brought home a gold medal. David offers fudge to go with this sweet wine. It is out of this world. Other outstanding wines are the DeChaunac, a red wine aged in oak, and his Orchard Blush, a semi-dry rhubarb wine. Watch for their annual Christmas Cookie Walk in December and their Renaissance fair debuting in June of 2001.

Anderson Orchard and Winery

430 E. U.S. 6
Valparaiso, IN 46383
Phone: (219) 464-4936
(800) 673-2384
Fax: (219) 548-9738

www.andersonvineyard.com

Open:
January-April 15: Closed on Mondays and one hour earlier during the winter months.
April – January: Mon-Sat 10 – 6
Sun: 11 – 5

Dune Ridge Winery

From Anderson Winery go south on IN-49 to IN-2 East to IN-94 West to US-20 (exit 22 B). The winery has a sign alerting travels where to turn in.

The Dune Ridge Winery was established in June 1998. It is family owned and operated by Ken and Kathy Holevinsky. The Holevinskys bought about one acre of wooded land in October 1995. There was also a 1940s vintage motor lodge on the property. They renovated the motor lodge and turned it into a tasting room, a wine cellar and a bottling/blending facility. Ken is a full-time engineer and Kathy manages the winery. But what makes this winery unusual is that both Ken and Kathy are winemakers. Kathy is the main winemaker at Dune Ridge. Kathy has a

B.S. in Microbiology and she applies her science background to her winemaking skills. Together, the Holevinskys produce 14 different wines. They buy their viniferas from California and their hybrids from Michigan.

Dune Ridge's most popular wine is Lakeshore Red, a sweet wine. With black cherry aromas, this wine is magnificent. It won the silver medal at the Indy International Competition in 1999 and 2000. Their Vidal Blanc semi-dry has a tropical, melon flavor. It won the silver medal at the Indy International Competition in 1998. The White Zinfandel won a bronze medal at the same competition in 2000, which is also the year of its debut. It has been a very popular choice since its arrival.

The Dune Ridge Winery is young and growing, producing 500 cases annually, and one should not underestimate its potential. Since opening in 1998, their wines have won 12 medals all together.

Dune Ridge Winery

1240 Beam Street
Porter, IN 46304
Phone: (219) 926-5532

www.duneridgewinery.com

Open:

Wed: 11– 5
Sun: Noon – 5
Weekends only, January through April

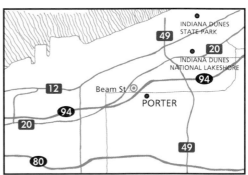

Lake Michigan Winery

Lake Michigan Winery is located in Whiting, Indiana, just six blocks from Lake Michigan, and one mile from Chicago. From Dune Ridge Winery, turn right on US-20, heading southwest. Take the I-94 West ramp to exit 2, US-41 South. Veer left at the fork in the ramp and merge onto Indianapolis Blvd/IN-152 North. IN-152 becomes US-20/US-12. Follow it, and then turn left onto 120th Street and go around the block to 119th Street.

It was the summer of 1986 that Tom Owens planted French hybrid grapevines just outside of Madison. He bought the hybrids from a New York vineyard and by the fall of 1989, there were enough grapes to harvest. However, after all the careful planning and harvesting, the vineyard was destroyed

three years later by an out-of-control grass fire which caused severe damage to the plants' posts and trellis system. He abandoned the vineyard and now purchases fruit from Michigan and California.

The winery has been described as funky and something that you would visit under the Brooklyn Bridge. It has two aging cellars below street level, and at the cellar entrance there are stained glass designs of wine

grapes. Once you step inside, the atmosphere is gay and festive with antiques and hanging baskets dangling from the ceiling of the small restaurant. The restaurant also has turn-of-the-century ice cream chairs and tables where you can enjoy a glass of wine with a cheese tray. They have a small garden and seating area that is perfect in the summer months. The winery has hog and lamb roasts, beefsteak cookouts, grape stomp festivals, hay rides for the kids and much more.

Lake Michigan Winery offers 20 selections of wines, which are mostly dry and semi-sweet options. The most popular are Cabaret Chicago or the Hammond Salmon, a dry white wine. From the California grapes, try the Zinfandel, a robust red with berry-like spicy flavors; the Pinot Noir; or the Chardonnay, with fruity characteristics of plums and raspberries.

Lake Michigan Winery

US 41 (Calumet Avenue)
At 119th St.
Whiting, IN 46394
Phone: (219) 659-9463
Fax: (219) 659-3501

www.lakemichiganwinery.com

Open:
Daily 1pm – 7pm

Satek Winery

This winery is new to the north.

Pam and Larry Satek (the name rhymes with attic) will start construction in late fall of 2000 on their new winery located on N. Van Guilder Rd. in Fremont, near the intersection of the Indiana Tollway and I-69. Satek Winery is the first commercial winery in northeastern Indiana and expects to open by Memorial Day, 2001.

Satek Winery is located on 16 acres and will house a production area and a tasting room as well as a picnic area. The first "crush" for the winery will take place in August of 2001. The wines available will include wine from the Sateks' 1999 and 2000 grape harvests– grown locally on two acres in Steuben County. The Sateks planted their first grapevines eight years ago on land located on the north shore of Lake James. Pam's great-grandfather used the same land for an apple orchard eighty years ago.

Larry Satek, the winery's master winemaker, is a research chemist who has been awarded 20 U.S. Patents. He is excited about combining his chemist's touch with his long time interest in winemaking. I look forward to the opening of this winery.

Satek Winery
6208 North Van Guilder Road
Fremont, IN 46737
Phone: (219) 833-9509

Northern Indiana Wineries and Their Communities

Dune Ridge Winery is in Porter County and Lake Michigan Winery and Anderson Winery are in Lake County.

Information

Porter County Convention and Visitors Bureau
800 Indiana Boundary Rd.
(219) 926-2255
(800) 283-TOUR

Lake County Convention and Visitors Bureau
5800 Broadway Street
Suite S
Merrillville, IN 46410
(219) 980-1617
(800) 255-5253

Places to Eat

Billy Jack's Café and Grill
2904 Calumet Ave.
(219) 462-3797

China House
120 E. Lincoln Way
(219) 462-5788

Strongbow Turkey Inn
Junction of State Road 49
and U.S. Highway 30
(219) 462-5121
(800) 462-5121

Wagner's Too
597 West U.S. Highway 30
(219) 759-6334

Places to Stay

Inn at Aberdeen
3158 South State Road 2
(219) 465-3753

Courtyard by Marriott
2301 E. Morthland Dr.
(219) 465-1700

Fairfield Inn
2101 E. Morthland Dr.
(219) 465-6225

Sights to See

Old Jail Museum,
Lake County
153 S. Franklin St.
(219) 465-3595

Carmelite Shrines
Lake County
1628 Ridge Road
(219) 838-9657

SS Constantine and Helen Greek Orthodox Cathedral
Lake County
(219) 769- 2481

Dunes State Nature Preserve
Porter County
1600 North 25 East
(219) 926-1952
See more different types of trees on 1,500 acres than you would see in any other area of the same size. Also see rare flowers and ferns, which are almost tropical, in the Midwest. There are campgrounds, a swimming beach and trails that are fit for all types of activities. This is a beautiful area–you must see it.

Events

Taste of Indiana
Whiting, June
(888) TNT-WINE or
(219) 659-WINE

Grape Stomp
Whiting, September
(888) TNT-WINE or
(219) 659-WINE

Taste of Porter
August (219) 926-4371 or
(219) 966-7217

41

Rockville

Terre Vin Winery

59

N

70

36

40

39
42
267
37 67

74

65

Chateau
Thomas
Winery

421

465

Gaia
Winery

Carmel

31

31

Easley Winery

Ferrin's Fruit
Winery

65

465

70

69

74

40

Central Indiana has five wineries. Our tour included Easley's, Gaia, Chateau Thomas, then out to Terre Vin and back to Carmel for Ferrin's. A new addition, Wilson's Winery in Modoc, is due to open in the Spring of 2001.

Covered Bridge, Parke County

Chateau Thomas Winery

The Chateau Thomas Winery is located in Cambridge Square on I-70, west of the Indianapolis Airport at Exit 66. Plenty of signs direct you to the winery even before you reach the exit. Head out for the Chateau before noon so you can have a plate of cheese or a sandwich while you taste the wine. Don't rush your visit, because there is a lot to take in at the 10,000-square-foot building. At first glance, the building looks like a new ware-house, except it has wine barrels that grace the exterior. Once you step inside, the building takes on a new life. The Chateau's tasting room features a unique round oak bar that resembles an oak barrel with real wine barrel strappings, which was designed by Dr. Thomas. A banquet room that seats 200 guests affords you a grand view of the oak barrels and stainless steel tanks and the entire production room. If you book the banquet room at the right time, you can enjoy watching the wonders of wine-making

Dr. Charles Thomas established the Chateau Thomas Winery in 1984. He wanted to produce wine from vinifera grapes (old world grapes) bought from Napa County, Oregon and Washington vineyards. The grapes are crushed on the West Coast, chilled to 34 degrees Fahrenheit and then shipped to the winery in one-ton bins by refrigerated truck. All of the winemaking process—from fermentation to bottling—is done at the Chateau.

Dr. Thomas, an ob-gyn, started making wine as a hobby in the early 1970s, with a wine kit he purchased from a local Indianapolis wine store. He and three friends organized the Indianapolis chapter of the American Society of Wine so they could taste and critique each other's wines. Soon, Dr. Thomas began teaching winemaking classes at IUPUI (Indiana University, Purdue University at Indianapolis). For several years, Dr. Thomas would fly out to California to buy crushed grapes and bring them back to Indianapolis. By 1983, he had enhanced his skills as a winemaker by enrolling at the Napa Valley School of Cellaring to take instruction from Bruce Rector. He flew to California every weekend for six months to attend these classes. After receiving his Certificate of Cellaring, Dr. Thomas opened a small winery in downtown, Indianapolis, and within nine years had expanded and moved his operation to Plainfield, Indiana. One year later, the Chateau opened a handsome tasting room in Nashville, Indiana.

Dr. Thomas uses old-world methods of winemaking in which the wines age slowly. The winery is known for its rich, full-bodied Cabernet Sauvignon and complex Merlots–and particularly for the 1996 Family Reserve, a Bordelais blend that has won three international medals. These austere wines are fermented on the skins for an average of 14 days, then pressed and aged in oak for two or more years.

While at the Chateau, you must try the 1989 Sauvignon Blanc, a French-style white wine with creamy oak textures. If you are a sweet wine drinker, try the 1998 Fleur d'Peche, a lovely, floral, light white wine with full, fruity

aromas on many levels. One of Dr. Thomas' trademark wines, the Fleur d'Peche has been honored with gold, silver and bronze medals. These wines are well worth sampling—over and over!

On a special note, the Chateau's wines have been served to the President and Vice President of the United States. They were also served at the 1994 National Democratic Governors' Conference Banquet, the Indiana Governor's Mansion and many other esteemed functions. Dr. Thomas is famous in the region for his wine seminars and the basic winemaking technique classes that he conducts at his winery.

Chateau Thomas Winery

6291 Cambridge Way
(I-70 & SR 267)
Plainfield, IN 46168-7904
Phone: (888) 761-WINE

www.chateauthomas.com

Open:
Mon–Thurs: 10am-9pm
Fri–Sat: 10am-10pm
Sun: Noon-7pm

Retail Store
225 S. Van Buren Street
SR 135, 1 block N. of SR 46
Nashville, IN 47448-1613
Phone: (800) 761-WINE

Open:
Mon–Thurs: 11am-5pm
Fri: 11am-8pm
Sat: 1pm-8pm
Sun: Noon-5pm

Terre Vin Winery

Mansfield Red

rom the Chateau, head west to the Terre Vin Winery in Rockville, this is the only winery in the West-Central Indiana area. Take State Road 267 south to State Road 36 west and head straight to Rockville–about 60 miles from the Chateau Thomas Winery. Once in Rockville, you will need to turn right at Jefferson Street, the first traffic light, and go one short block to Terre Vin Winery. You can't miss it.

Dave and Dorothy Gahimer established the Terre Vin Winery in 1995. Dave is the winery's winemaker and Dorothy is in charge of operations.

Before opening their winery, Dave and Dorothy led another kind of lifestyle. Dave was a technician and Dorothy worked in the library at Indiana State University. It was when the Gahimers' son-in-law gave Dave a winemaking kit that he began to make homemade wines. After many years of teaching himself how to perfect the trade, Dave made a career change and turned his love of making wines into a business. The Gahimers obtained their license in July, 1995, and opened their doors for wine production in a small 24 x 36-foot room under their garage. Within two years, they moved their establishment to Terre Haute. They leased a 5,000-square-foot former supermarket and turned it into Terre Vin Winery, complete with wine production, a tasting room and a special room for meetings and events. This is a low-key, no frills winery that is still in the making. However, people who know of this winery come for the superb Cabernet Sauvignon Meritage, a truly successful blending of wines

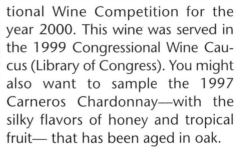

with deep, aromatic fruit. This was a Bronze Medal winner in the San Francisco International Wine Competition for the year 2000. This wine was served in the 1999 Congressional Wine Caucus (Library of Congress). You might also want to sample the 1997 Carneros Chardonnay—with the silky flavors of honey and tropical fruit— that has been aged in oak.

In 1998, the Gahimers added a new label to their wine list–the Sainte Marie des Bois Cabernet Sauvignon Meritage. This is a blend of grapes with Cabernet Sauvignon and Cabernet Franc from Sonoma Valley and Merlot from Yakima Valley, Washington, all of which are aged in American oak. The wine is vinted at Terre Vin Winery by associate winemaker John Heck under his Sainte Marie des Bois label. This was the first Meritage wine released in Indiana. Only 30 wineries are licensed to use the name Meritage on their wine labels to designate a wine blended from varieties of Bordeaux grapes. Meritage represents the art of blending, and no single variety may make up more than 90 percent of the blend.

Terre Vin Winery

100 W. York Street
Rockville, IN 47872
Phone: (888) 965-WINE
Fax: (765) 569-5199

www.ticz.com/~terrevin

Open:
Mon–Sat: 11am-5pm
Sun: Noon-5pm

Gaia Wines

Gaia Wines, Inc., (pronounced guy' a), is named for the Greek goddess of the earth. Gaia is located in downtown Indianapolis at 608 Massachusetts Avenue, right in the middle of the theater district. Gaia opened its doors for wine tasting and selling in 1996.

Gaia winery is owned by Angee Walberry, the first woman to own and operate a winery in the state of Indiana. More importantly, Gaia is the only woman-owned winery among the 1,700 wineries located in the United States. Walberry is the winemaker at Gaia, which currently offers 13 wines, many of which have won awards.

The winery is located in the up-and-coming arts district in Indianapolis. The winery fits right into this upbeat section of town. Gaia's interior is the most unique of the Indiana wineries. Wall sconces from the old Realto building in downtown Indianapolis adorn its brick walls. Two copper tasting bars and three wonderful chandeliers from Indianapolis' former L.S. Ayres downtown store complete the eclectic effect. The interior alone is worth the stop. While you are on the Avenue, stop for dinner at Agio's restaurant for a great dish of pasta.

Angee Walberry received her certification as a Cellarmaster with the International Wine Academy and has been making wine since 1990. With a degree in chemistry from Indiana University, Walberry came by winemaking quite naturally–experimenting with the blending of different fruits became an extension of her training in science. Walberry balances her love of winemaking with her interest

in clinical social work. She is the Managed Care Director in the Department of Psychiatry at IUPUI.

While you are at Gaia, try the buttery Chardonnay, with a hint of ripe apple and melon. It has also been honored with well-deserved 1998 Great Lakes Gold and 1998 Indy International Competition Gold awards. The rich Merlot is a delight to drink when young–this dry red should not be missed. The sweet wine lover should try the Indianapolis Red–a Hoosier favorite made with native Midwest Concord grapes.

Gaia's labels are unique. Rendered by artist R.J. Hohimer, each of the labels' drawings sport a title and watercolor unrelated to the winery or vineyards. Don't miss their Web site for annual events such as the Fall Harvest, which is the third Saturday in September, and the Elegant Eve, a New Year's Eve dinner and party.

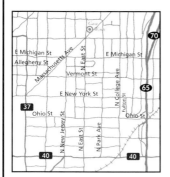

Gaia Winery

608 Massachusetts Avenue
Indianapolis, IN 46024
Phone: (317) 634-WINE

www.gaiawines.com

Open:
Mon–Sat: opens at 11am
Sun: Noon - 6pm

Easley Winery

Easley Winery, the second oldest winery in Indiana, is located in downtown Indianapolis, right off Ohio Street. Its vineyards are in Cape Sandy, Indiana. The vineyards are high on the southern slopes of the Ohio River, where they can take advantage of the most sunlight and cooler night temperatures from the river, along with maximum drainage.

Attorney John Easley turned his interest in winemaking into a hobby in the 1960s, even flying out to California to take a few winemaking classes from the University of California at Davis. His hobby began to take a serious turn when he and a group of other professionals joined together in an effort to  change the Indiana wine laws which prohibited winemaking and the selling of those wines in Indiana. By 1971, the law had changed and commercial winemaking had become a legal option.

In 1970, John Easley bought 50 acres in anticipation of the law passing and began planting French hybrids (American labrusca and European vinifera grapes). It takes two to three years to actually produce the French hybrid grapes. In 1974, the Easleys purchased an old ice cream factory building in downtown Indianapolis. Their winery is still there. In the early 1990s, Indiana went through some very harsh winters and almost half of the Easley vineyards froze. Today they harvest 18 acres of French hybrid vines such as Chambourcin,

Chardonel, Foch, Chancellor and American Catawba–these varieties can withstand the harsh Indiana winters. They also contract with neighbors for additional acres for growing grapes.

When the grapes have been harvested, they are rushed to the winery for production. Easley Winery is different from the other Indiana wineries because their focus is more on the vineyards and wine production and less on the commercial winery. They only produce around 9,000 gallons of wine for their own winery. The rest of the juice is sold to home winemakers and other wineries, or they make wines to sell on the open market.

Son Mark Easley is the winery's winemaker. He grew up in the business of winemaking and is the second generation of winemakers in his family. Mark began working with his father at a very young age and became serious about the work in the early 1980s, ultimately becoming the winery's main winemaker. Until recently, however, Mark focused on the vineyards and growing the grapes while his father focused on winemaking. When his father died in 1997, Mark became the head winemaker and his wife, Meredith, became the director of sales and promotion.

One of Easley's best sellers, and the house specialty, is its old family recipe of warm mulled wine–an all-natural, full-bodied, red wine that has honey, lemon juice, apple cider and spices added to it. Served warm, it is especially good for the holidays or cold Indiana winters.

The Pink Catawba, similar to a White Zinfandel, is a light, slightly sweet, fruity pink wine made with American labrusca grapes. Another wine made from the labrusca grape is the Fredonia, a fruity, silky red wine. Easley makes consistently good Chancellor Noir, an outstanding dry, heavy-bodied, tannin-rich red wine. Some call this Indiana's Merlot.

Easley Winery

205 N. College Avenue
Indianapolis, IN 46202
Phone and Fax: (317) 636-4516

Open:
Mon-Fri: 9am-6pm
Sat: 9am-5pm
Sun: Noon-4pm

Ferrin's Fruit Winery

Located at 89 1st Avenue on the beautiful tree-lined streets of Old Towne Carmel is the newly opened Ferrin's Fruit Winery. To get there, you take U.S. 31 North (North Meridian Street) to 116th Street. Turn right on 116th, then left on Rangeline Road. On Rangeline, you will go north to Main Street (also known as 131st Street). Take a left on Main Street and another left onto 1st Avenue S.W.

Owned by David and Mary Ann Ferrin, this winery not only specializes in wines made from fruits, jams and jellies, but also has some very good dry wines.

For 35 years, David worked as an electrical engineer at WTHR-TV (Channel 13). Then, in 1996, he went to buy a wine rack and came home with an entire winemaking kit instead. He bought a recipe book that showed how to make wine from fruits and jellies. David began to experiment. He made wine from kiwis, pumpkins, blueberries–even raisins and carrots! Finally, almost 350 bottles later, David was ready to turn his hobby into a career. He bought a small commercial building in Carmel and spent months renovating it.

One unique aspect of Ferrin's Fruit Winery is the gift shop. They sell wine accessories like other wineries, but they also provide specialty gifts. There is David's Black Cherry Vinegar–a wonderful oil and vinegar salad dressing. They also have something for your pets like Sauvi-

gnon Bark Dog Treats, Meow Merlot Cat Treats and even Bordeaux Peep Birdseed!

The Desert Lily white wine is one of three that is made traditionally, from grapes. It is smooth and melon-like, with a nutty flavor. Ferrin's Vineyard Passion, also made from grapes, is a supple, spicy red wine that won the silver medal at the Indy International Wine Competition.

Ferrin's Fruit Winery

89 1st Avenue SW
(Southwest corner of Rangeline Road and Main Street)
Carmel, IN 46032
Phone: (317) 566-9463

Open:
Tue–Sat: 11am-7pm
Sun: Noon-5pm (Carry-Out on Sunday)

Central Indiana Wineries and Their Communities

Rockville

Information

Parke County Convention and Visitors Bureau
401 East Ohio Street
Rockville, IN 47872
(765) 569-5226

Places to Stay

Knoll Inn-Distinctive
Suites Bed and Breakfast
317 West High Street
(765) 569-6345

Owl Nest Bed and Breakfast
303 Howard Avenue
(765) 569-1803

Events & Sights

Turkey Run State Park
Rocky Hollow/Falls Canyon State National Preserve
The Narrow Bridge
Billie Creek Village Museum
Covered Bridge Festival
(Parke County is considered to be the covered bridge capital of the world.)
Late Winter Maple Fair
Vintage Indiana Wine and Food Festival–June 10th
A Taste of Indiana–August 3rd

Downtown Indianapolis

There are many restaurants and events in and around Indianapolis. We are unable to list them all.

Information

Indianapolis City Center
Pan Am Plaza
201 South Capitol Avenue
(800) 323-4639
(317) 237-5206

Places to Eat

Alcatraz Brewing Co.
Circle Centre,
49 West Maryland Street
(317) 488-1230
Located near the newest mall in Indianapolis, this brewery offers several of its own delicious specialty beers.

Agio
635 Massachusetts Avenue
(317) 488-0359
A wonderful and fun Italian restaurant! Great wine list, too.

Bazbeaux
334 Massachusetts Avenue
(317) 636-7662
Unique sandwiches and some of the best pizza in town.

Dunaway's
351 South East Street
(317) 638-7663
If you are planning a romantic night out, the Italian cuisine and large wine list will definitely help set the mood.

Indiana Bread Co.
6 W. Washington Street
(317) 972-1215
For lunch or breakfast, the Bread Co. is completely casual and you can't beat the value.

Hot Tuna
Omni Severin Hotel
40 West Jackson Place
(317) 687-5190
Especially popular for its seafood, this restaurant is a favorite of the locals. While you're there, check out the amenities that the hotel has to offer. It's worth your time.

Something Different
4939 East 82nd Street,
(317) 570-7700
(317) 570-4668
Very fine dinning with an exceptional menu that changes monthly.

Where to Stay

Old Northside Bed and Breakfast
1340 North Alabama Street
(317) 635-9123

The Hoffman House
545 East 11th Street
(317) 635-1701

Radisson Hotel City Centre
31 West Ohio Street
(800) 333-3333

Omni Severin Hotel
40 West Jackson Place
(800) 843-6664

The Westin Hotel
50 South Capitol Avenue
(800) 228-3000

Northern Indianapolis and Carmel

Information

Hamilton County Convention and Visitors Bureau
11601 Municipal Drive
(317) 598-4444

Carmel Clay Chamber of Commerce
41 E. Main Street
(317) 846-1049

Places to Eat

Loon Lake Lodge
6880 E. 82nd Street
(317) 845-9011

With animals popping out of every corner, it's no wonder that people "flock" here.

Illusions
969 Keystone Way
(317) 575-8312

Enjoy a truly magical evening, thanks to the restaurant's own magicians.

Tavola di Tosa
6523 Ferguson Avenue
(317) 202-0240

They import 80% of their food from Italy. Call for reservations well in advance.

Corner Wine Bar
6331 N. Guilford Avenue
(317) 255-5159

Places to Stay

Doubletree Guest Suites
11355 N. Meridian Street
(317) 844-7994

Frederick-Talbott Inn at the Prairie
Bed and Breakfast
13805 Allisonville Road
(317) 578-3600

Camel Lot Bed and Breakfast
4512 W. 131st Street
(317) 873-4370

Accommodations are very unique, with a camellia tree growing in each suite. Also on the grounds are zebras, llamas, deer and 2 Siberian tigers.

Sights to See

Conner Prairie Pioneer Settlement
13400 Allisonville Road
(800) 966-1836

"Residents" perform daily tasks of the 1800s. Conner Prairie received 4 stars for authenticity from U.S. News and World Report *magazine.*

Events

Indianapolis Wine Festival—June
(sponsored by the Indiana Wine Grape Council.)

Indy International Wine Competition, Indiana State Fair—August
(sponsored by the Indiana Wine Grape Council.)

Penrod Arts Fair—September
(317) 923-1331

Village Tour of Homes—October
(765) 873-3836

Where to Buy Wine

Grapevine Cottage
120 S. Main Street
Zionsville, IN 46077

Wonderful selection of wines and gourmet items.

Marsh Supermarkets
Kahn's Fine Wines
Hamilton Beverage
United Package Liquors
Wild Oats
The Liquor Shoppe

On this tour there are five wineries, all centered in Bloomington and Nashville, except for Simmons, which is located in Columbus. Bloomington and Nashville are popular tourist areas where you will see some of the most beautiful natural limestone and luscious hills in Indiana. Most of these wineries have or will have estate wines from their vineyards. Our tour includes Oliver Winery, Butler Winery, Chateau Thomas Tasting Room, Brown County Winery, Simmons Winery and Vineyard and Shadey Lake Winery.

Oliver Winery's Creekbend Vineyard

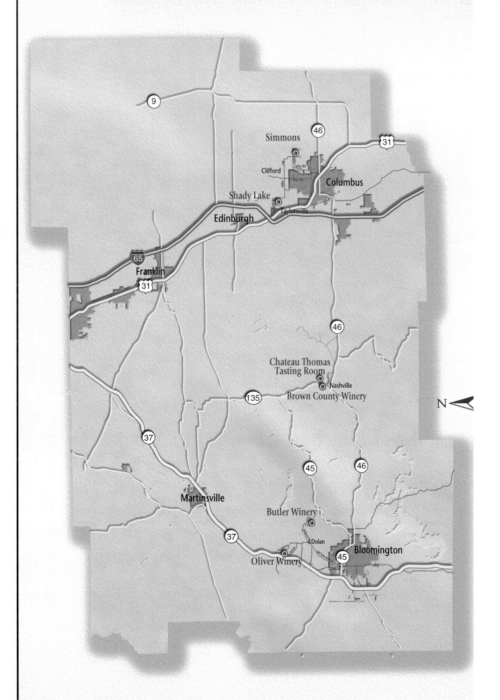

9

46

31

Simmons

Clifford

Valley Rd

Main Rd

Columbus

Shady Lake

Edinburgh

Taylorsville

65

Franklin

31

46

Chateau Thomas
Tasting Room

Nashville

135

Brown County Winery

N

37

45

46

Martinsville

Butler Winery

Dolan

Old State Rd 37

Oliver Winery

45

Bloomington

Oliver Winery and Vineyard

Begin your wine trek in South Central Indiana with Oliver Winery. From Indianapolis, follow State Road 37 South and this will take you right to the Oliver Winery. There are several road signs on your right alerting you to its location. This winery is not to be missed.

There is nothing sweet and quaint about Oliver Winery–it is big and beautifully laid out, graced with Indiana limestone built into waterfalls and monoliths, all surrounded by carefully manicured grounds. The winery is nestled into the surrounding limestone and sculptures with a hacienda-like look, complete with wooded arches and a veranda that surrounds the winery. The wine tasting room is a large, timber-

framed room made with high beamed oak and poplar. The interior sports two grand wine counters to serve the many people who flock to Oliver Winery. On an average weekend, the winery will see around 2,000 customers. The tasting room opens up to a spectacular garden and pond, deep enough to launch a rowboat. There is always plenty to eat at the winery, from fresh baguettes to an assortment of cheeses and many gourmet products. You can also drink your wine and eat lunch while sitting out on the veranda. The Olivers have pur-

posely made the winery very comfortable for customers to come and stay a long time.

William W. Oliver, an Indiana University law professor, began making wine in his basement in the early 1960s. In 1963, while on a teaching sabbatical, Professor Oliver visited some wineries and vineyards in Ithaca, New York. Immediately upon his return to Indiana, he bought land in northern Monroe County and planted five acres of French-American hybrid grapes. Grape production exceeded all his expectations.

Professor Oliver and other fledgling winemakers could not sell their wines to the public—only to wholesalers. He decided to write the Indiana Small Winery Act in 1971, which was passed by the state legislature. This new law allowed small wineries to produce up to 100,000 gallons of wine for annual wholesale and retail sales in Indiana. The new law also allowed Indiana-produced wine to be sold on Sundays.

By the spring of 1972, Professor Oliver opened his winery for business. He began with four wines and 35 acres of wine grapes. However, it was purchasing the rights to Camelot Mead that put Oliver Winery on the map in Indiana. While at the University of California at Davis,

Professor Oliver met Ernie Lane, with whom he purchased the formula and the exclusive rights to make the honey wine. Within five years, Camelot Mead was Oliver Winery's biggest seller and, consequently, the winery's biggest percentage of wine production. Still, Professor Oliver's main profession was as a law professor and winemaking was a hobby for him until he retired in 1983.

When Professor Oliver retired, the winery was seeing red and the family sold some of the property to pay off the debt to keep the winery going. Professor Oliver asked his son if he wanted the failing business. Bill attended winemaking classes and seminars and slowly began learning the trade, all while attending the MBA program at Indiana University in Bloomington.

Bill was not alone in his dream to make a successful business out of the failing winery. Kathleen Oliver, a California native (now married to Bill), was attending the MBA program with Bill and together they began cleaning up the vineyard and creating a marketing plan for the winery. In 1993, Kathleen came on board as the general manager and Bill became the president. Kathleen's job is running the retail component while Bill's is to focus on the production side of the business. Bill and Kathleen recently purchased a 117-acre farm next to their vineyard and they plan to plant 15 acres of wine grapes a year until they reach 60 acres of wine grapes for production. Bill and Kathleen are worth keeping an eye on as their plans for the future of this winery evolve and unfold.

At present time, they have five acres of wine grapes at their Creekbend Vineyards: Caber-

net Sauvignon, Cabernet Franc, Chardonel, Marechal Foch (their nouveau wine) and a numbered wine, NY70.809 (this is soon-to-be named). They presently produce over 150,000 gallons of wine, or 63,091 cases, annually.

From their Creekbed Vineyard estate-bottled wines, try Oliver's Marechal Foch Nouveau 1999 and 2000. Both years are quite good. Fans of Merlot will find this wine rich, smooth and loaded with fruit. Please take note of the label: It is of their young son's footprint–very original! (The 2000 Nouveau has two foot-prints, in anticipation of their new child on the way.) A bottle of this wine would be great at the winery's picnic grounds that overlook the pond. Their estate Chardonnel, with a buttery apricot aroma, is well worth the visit to Oliver's. Or try the estate Cabernet Sauvignon, particularly the 1997, with strong tannins and tons of fruit. They have many variations to try–from the very dry Gewürztraminer and Blaufrankish, to the very sweet wines such as the Muscat Canelli or Camelot Mead. Whatever your taste is, Oliver Winery has something for everyone.

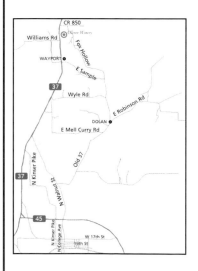

Oliver Winery
8024 North State Road 37
Bloomington, IN 47404
Phone: (812) 876-5800
Fax: (812) 876-9309

Open:
Mon–Sat: 10–6
Sun: Noon–6

Tours:
Fri–Sat: Noon–4:30
Sun: 1–4:30 (every half-hour)
Cellar Tours: Friday-Sunday afternoons

UPS Shipping is FREE when purchasing in multiples of 6 bottles.

Butler Winery and Vineyard

Butler Winery
BLUEBERRY
Table Wine

The Butler Winery and Vineyard is a very short drive from Oliver Winery. Here you will taste some of the best Chambourcin ever made. From Oliver's, turn left (south) on S.R.37, then take an immediate left (east) onto Sample Road. (Look for Wylie Floor Coverings Warehouse at the intersection.) Follow Sample Road until it ends at Old 37 and go right for about two miles on a curvy road. Take the first left on Robinson Road and go about 3 1/2 miles–you will see a sign that says Butler Vineyards on the right. As you travel through the winding road flush with multi-colored foliage in a heavily wooded area, you will soon reach the Butlers' well-manicured vineyards. Off to the side is the newly built tasting and production room. Don't expect a grand setting–it's not their style. These rooms are Quaker style with high beams and little fluff and fanfare. This winery is all about making wine.

I also recommend that you head to Bloomington to visit their wine tasting room. You will most likely find Jim pouring and selling the wine, and if you want information on any wine, he will be glad to discuss anything with you. From Butler Vineyards, head to Bloomington on S.R.37 South to the College/Walnut Exit. Go straight through three stoplights

after exiting. The third stoplight is 17th Street. The next cross street is 15th Street and the Winery is on the left at 15th and College. Look

for a lovely, white turn-of-the-century home. There is a large sign in front, so you can't miss it.

Jim and Susie Butler opened Butler Winery 17 years ago. However, unlike most of the winemakers in Indiana, Jim did not start out making wine as a hobby. He started as an assistant winemaker at Oliver Winery over 20 years ago.

Jim was a doctoral candidate in the Freshwater Biology program at Indiana University in the late 1970s. There was a recession in this country at that time and jobs were hard to get, particularly in his specialized field. He landed a job at Oliver Winery as an assistant winemaker and began learning the winemaking trade. With his knowledge of chemistry, winemaking came easily for him and he soon moved up to head winemaker. Needless to say, he stayed in the wine business and dropped out of the Freshwater Biology program.

After working six years for Oliver Winery, the Butlers established their own winery in 1983. Jim started by making his wine in the cellar of their turn-of-the-century home in Bloomington. He would sell it from the front of the house. Jim, Susie and their three children lived upstairs. Their voluminous wine production soon squeezed them out of their home, but it was also time to set up their own estate. They bought a house with some land on a winding hilltop in Monroe County, just nine miles from Bloomington. They had agreed that they could make better wines from their own grapes, and at a lower cost. By 1992, they had planted 3.5 acres of wine grapes–Vignoles, Chardonel and Chambourcin. The vineyard produces more than half of the wine sold at

Butler Winery and they supplement the shortage with grapes that come from Indiana. For the year 2000, the vineyard will have produced 2,000 cases of wine.

From the Butlers' estate, the prize-winning 1998 Chambourcin is an excellent dry, yet smooth red wine that lingers on the palate. The 1999 Chardonel, a white wine with an almondy aroma, is a must-try. This year is the first vintage of Chardonel from their vineyard. You don't want to miss the White Select, a smooth, rich and creamy wine made from Seyval grapes and a winner of a gold medal at the Indy International Wine Competition.

Jim Butler is one of the few winemakers in Indiana who produces sparkling wines. He turns Seyval Blanc grapes into delicious bubbly using the champenoise method.

Butler Tasting Room

1022 N. College Avenue (15th & College)
Bloomington, IN 47404
Phone/Fax: (812) 339-7233

Email: vineyard@BlueMarble.net
www.butlerwinery.com

Open:
Mon–Sat: 10am–6pm
Sun: Noon–6pm

Butler Winery & Vineyard

6200 East Robinson Road
Bloomington, IN 47408

Brown County Winery

F rom Butler Winery's Tasting Room, head to Nashville. Take a left on College (south) to 3rd Street. Turn left (east) on 3rd Street and follow it until it veers to the right into Atwater. Follow Atwater to Eastside Drive. Go left on Eastside, back to 3rd Street. Go right onto 3rd Street, heading east, which turns into IN-46. Follow IN-46 about 16 miles until you hit Nashville, then head north on SR135 (Nashville's main street.) The winery is in the middle of the town on Old School Way. It looks like a back alley, but it is actually a street. You can't miss it. They have recently built a larger, more beautiful winery just outside of Nashville and they are using the in-town winery as a tasting room only.

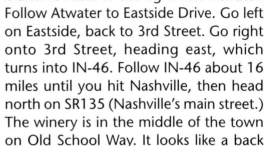

David Schrodt began his career as a winemaker in 1982, working at Oliver Winery. In 1986, David and his wife, Cynthia, opened the Brown County Winery in Nashville, Indiana. He is now the head winemaker for Brown County Winery. Cynthia, on the other hand, was in a much different field. She was the Executive Director of the Girls Incorporated Social Service Agency. She quit in 1994 to manage the retail components of the winery full-time.

Now, 14 years after their beginning, the Schrodts have another wine facility just east of Nashville—a spacious production room and a beautiful designer-quality tasting room. The exceptional bar is topped with limestone, while the rest is made of natural poplar. This room makes you want to linger and taste until you can taste no longer. It also has two large picture windows that overlook the pro-

duction room, so you can sip and watch the winemaking process. If you are lucky, Dave will be around to answer any questions that you might have.

Since Brown County Winery does not have its own vineyard, the Schrodts must purchase their grapes from suppliers in Michigan, Southern Indiana and New York. For their dry wines, they use grapes from French-American hybrids. A good wine to try from these hybrids would be the Autumn Red, a dry red with soft tannins, and the Autumn White, a buttery melon-edged wine. Both wines won the bronze medal at the Indy International Competition in 2000. Still, the Schrodts are best known for their berry dessert wines. The strawberry wine has actually won gold medals four years in a row. Obviously, this one should be on the top of your list to try.

Brown County Winery

P.O. Box 450 (Old School Way)
Nashville, IN 47448
Phone: (812) 988-6144
Fax: (812) 988-8285

Open:
Mon–Sat: 10am–5:30pm
Sun: Noon–5:30pm

The new winery is located east of Nashville on IN-46.

Chateau Thomas
Tasting Room

From Old School Way in Nashville, walk about two blocks north to Coachlight Square. You can't miss it. This is Chateau Thomas Winery's second location in Indiana. It is a beautiful tasting room with gourmet foods and Indiana cheeses to buy. It's wonderful to get off your feet and taste some wine before dinner or after shopping. The winery has a great terrace where you can sit and sip your glass of wine.

Chateau Thomas Winery
225 South Van Buren Street
Nashville, IN 47448
Phone: (812) 988-8500
(800) 761-WINE

www.chateauthomas.com

Simmons Winery

From the Chateau Thomas Winery in Nashville, drive to the Simmons Winery in Columbus, Indiana. To get there, get back on IN-46 heading east to Columbus, approximately 24 miles. Go left onto IN-9 and go about three miles to CR-450 North, also known as Hope Road. Turn left and the winery will be on your right.

This is another brand new winery and vineyard, owned by David and Brenda Simmons. The winery is nestled in between vineyards and farmland. This new estate is worth keeping your eye on. The vineyard is on the 115-

year-old family farm, which has been producing vegetables for the past 50 years on 900 acres. However, growing wine grapes is a new venture for David. The vineyard began with 4 acres in 1998 and he planted another 4 1/2 in the spring of 1999. Since it will take about three years for the vineyard to fully develop, David does not expect a full harvest until about 2003. David and Brenda built their winery and Brenda built all of the shelving on the interior. It is small, yet very pleasant.

The wine business is part of Brenda's family history. Her grandparents grew grapes and her father made wine. Brenda is a retired mathematics teacher and now she manages the winery and vineyard with David. However, Brenda kept her position as coach of the Columbus North High School girls' basketball team.

From their purchased grapes, David's Merlot is good– with a full-bodied taste and hints of berry flavors. The Vidal Blanc, a semi-sweet white wine, is a real treat for any wine lover and worthy of respect.

Simmons Winery

8111 E. 450 North
Columbus, IN 47203
Phone: (812) 546-0091

Open:
Mon–Sat: 10am–6pm
Sun: Noon–5pm

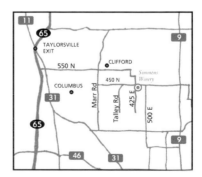

Shadey Lake Winery

From Simmons Winery, take I-65 South to exit 76A (Highway 31 South). At the first traffic light, turn left onto Tannehill Road. They are located 1/4 mile down the road on the left.

Greg and Pam Schmeltz are the owners of this newly established winery. They opened their business in October 2000. The Shadey Lake Winery specializes in dry to semi-dry fruit wines. They offer strawberry, blackberry and dry cherry table wines. Not seen on many menus is their Black Raspberry Table Wine, a full-bodied fruit wine with flavors of raspberries, cherries and blackberries. This is an excellent dessert wine.

At the moment they buy their grapes from around Indiana and Michigan. Greg is the winemaker and Pam manages the winery.

Shadey Lake Winery

1440 Tannehill Road
Taylorsville, IN 47280
Phone: (812) 526-0294

www.shadeylakewinery.com

Open:
Sat 10am–6pm
Sun: Noon–5pm

South Central Indiana Wineries and Their Communities

Bloomington

Information

Monroe County Convention and Visitors Bureau
2855 North Walnut Street
Bloomington, IN 47404
(800) 800-0037

Places to Eat

The Runcible Spoon
(restaurant/café)
412 East Sixth Street
(812) 334-3997

Owned by Jeff Danielson, The Runcible Spoon is an ethnic journey worth taking. Customers can sit upstairs, downstairs or outside in a lovely Japanese garden. Enjoy many different types of food from Seoul barbecue to African Groundnut Soup to homemade bagels. While you wait for your food, enjoy the 300-gallon aquarium on the main floor. For even more fish, check out the bathtub in the restroom-it also doubles as an aquarium. Brunch is served on Sunday.

The Trojan Horse
Southeast corner of Kirkwood and Walnut Street
(812) 332-1101

The Trojan Horse is known for their gyros. They also offer Greek salads and pastries.

Peterson's
1811 East Tenth Street
(In the Crosstown Shopping Center)
(812) 336-5450

Known for their fruit-flavored yogurt smoothies, Peterson's is very popular among locals and tourists alike.

Places to Stay

Grant Street Inn
310 North Grant Street
(812) 334-2353
24 Rooms

Indiana Memorial Union Hotel
900 East Seventh Street
(812) 856-6381
186 Rooms

Scholars Inn-Bed and Breakfast
801 North College Avenue
(812) 332-1892
6 Rooms

Pubs, Clubs and Sports Bars

Mars Nightclub
419 N. Walnut Street
(812) 332-0402
Enjoy a full bar, live music and dancing.

Irish Lion
212 W. Kirkwood Avenue
(812) 339-9076
Experience Irish music, Irish food and outdoor dining.

The Brewpub at Lennie's
419 Walnut Street
(812) 332-0402
Come here for gourmet pizza, handcrafted ales and a full menu.

Nick's
423 E. Kirkwood Avenue
(812) 332-4040
If you want large screen TVs, drinks, pool tables and a full menu, then this is the place to be.

Uncle Elizabeth's
201 S. College Avenue
(812) 331-0060
For a bit of a twist on your evening, come to this piano bar, which also offers outdoor seating, pool tables and a full bar.

Sights to See

Rose Hill Cemetery

On the western edge of Bloomington–use the Elm Street entrance.

This cemetery is often referred to as a "stone garden," because the gravestones have many wonderful pictures, such as weeping willows, carved into them. The weeping willow was a common symbol of grief in the 1800s. Some of the gravestones date back to the Civil War. The older markers are made of marble, while the newer ones are made of Indiana limestone. This is the final resting place of many interesting people such as composer Hoagy Carmichael, Alfred Kinsey and even a former Civil War general. One very interesting memorial in the cemetery belongs to John B. Crafton. While in Europe, he became homesick and decided to take an early boat home to see his family in Bloomington. This boat happened to be the infamous Titanic. Unfortunately, Mr. Crafton was not one of the lucky survivors.

Morgan-Monroe State Forest

6220 Forest Road
Martinsville, IN 46151
(317) 342-4026

Go north from Bloomington on State Road 37 into the forest just before the Morgan-Monroe County Line to experience 23,916 acres of nature's beauty. This forest is also home to Draper's Cabin, which is about as far away from the conveniences of society as you can get. At only $10.50 per night, the renter cannot expect a lot of amenities.

Events

Little 500 Bicycle Race
Taste of Bloomington–June
Hoosier Fest–August
Bloomington Early Music Festival–May

Listen to different types of music, including baroque and classical.

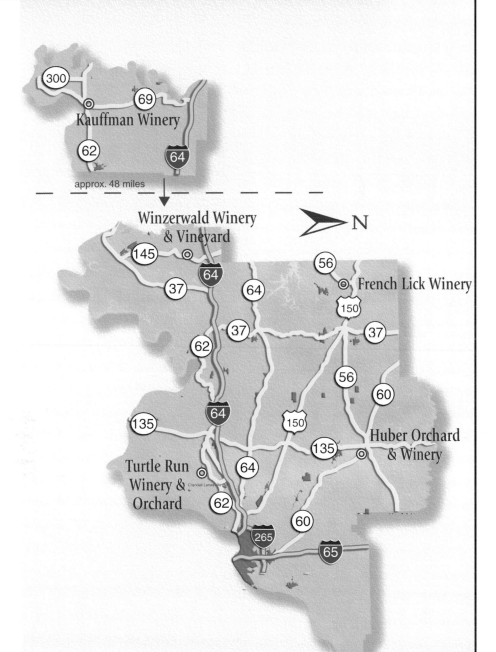

300

69

Kauffman Winery

62

64

approx. 48 miles

Winzerwald Winery
& Vineyard

N

145

64

37

64

56

French Lick Winery

150

37

37

62

56

60

64

150

135

64

Huber Orchard
& Winery

135

Turtle Run
Winery &
Orchard

Crandall Lanesville Rd.

64

62

60

265

65

We divided the Southern Indiana tour into two parts: the first tour is in the area of Orange County/French Lick. The two available wineries are French Lick and Hubers. Due to open in March, 2001 are Winzerwald Winery and Turtle Run. Kauffman Winery is not open to the public.

The second tour moves west to the Madison area. The Ohio River Valley is the only designated viticultural area in Indiana (as decreed by the Bureau of Alcohol, Tobacco and Firearms, or ATF). Consequently, most of the Indiana estates are located in the south.

French Lick Vineyard

French Lick Winery

For the first southern trek, start off at French Lick Winery. From Indianapolis, take SR-37 South to US 150 West. Exit on SR-56 East toward French Lick.

This winery is housed in the back of a magnificently restored Beechwood Mansion built in 1915 by the millionaire gambler, Ed Ballard. It is now a five bedroom bed and breakfast. French Lick Winery uses the Beechwood Mansion on their labels and even name their wines after its significant features.

John and Kim Doty opened their winery in 1995. They lease the mansion's 3,000-square-foot basement as a cellar for their wine production facility, as well as the small solarium upstairs that has an attached patio with tables to sit at while sipping the wine.

John and Kim are residents of Huntingburg. John is a loan officer at the First Bank of Huntingburg and Kim is the Holland, Indiana postmaster. They maintain their full-time jobs while still managing to run a winery and produce 20 different wines. To help out, their teenage sons give a hand in the summer months and some of their co-workers will lend a hand in the vineyard. John, the master winemaker, learned to make wine from his grandfather on their farm. Kim is the cellarmaster and a certified wine judge–she often participates in wine judging. As she says, "Nothing gets past my nose."

In 1994, The Dotys bought 40 acres of Kim's over-100-year-old family farm and began growing their own wine grapes on three of those acres. They have Norton, Vidal, Chambourcin, Chardonel, Vincent and Munson varieties. This year they will produce estate wine from their first plantings of Norton grapes.

By 1996, the Dotys were winning medals at the international competitions, particularly for their sweet Elderberry wine–a dark red wine with full elderberry aromas. Kim says that family members crawl through briars to find the elderberries used in their top-winning Beechwood Mansion wine. Try the Sey-val Blanc, a barrel fermented dry white with richness and complexity, carrying aromas of pineapple, citrus and toasted oak. The Dotys' 1997 Cabernet Sauvignon is a robust red with cherry, vanilla and elderberry nuances and was a silver medal winner at the 2000 Indy International Competition. I particularly enjoyed their Pinot Noir full of fruit flavors and a hint of pepper with a long after taste. It is a must-try!

French Lick Winery

8498 West State Road 56
French Lick, IN 47432
Phone: (812) 936-2293
(888) 494-6380

Email: flwinery@psci.net

Open:
March–December
Tues–Thurs: Noon–5pm
Fri–Sat: Noon–8pm
Sun: Noon–5pm

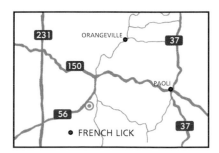

Huber Orchard and Winery

From French Lick to Huber Orchard and Winery, start out by going north on IN-56 toward US-150 by turning left. Enter the next roundabout and take 1st exit onto US-150/IN-56. Stay straight to go onto IN-56.

Turn right onto IN-135. Enter the next roundabout and take the first exit onto IN-135/IN-60. Turn left onto IN-60/South Jackson Street. This street turns into IN-60. Turn right onto Dow Knob Road.

The Huber Winery is not just a winery. There is a petting zoo with pony rides for kids, a farm market with produce from their own orchard and a cheese factory/shop! Plan to spend the day here. This is a beautiful winery—surrounded by majestic trees with colors of gold, wine and pumpkin—with ponds, picnic tables, the orchard and the animals! It is truly a lot to take in.

The Huber brothers are the 6th generation of Hubers to make wine. The winemaking in the Huber family began in 1843, with Simon Huber. Simon immigrated to Indiana from Germany and bought 80 acres of farmland for grapes and fruit. They now have over 600 acres, 35 of which are devoted to French hybrid grapes like the Seyval Blanc, Vignoles, Vidal and native American grapes such as Niagara and Concord. The Hubers are Indiana's largest wine producers. Their vineyards produce over 25,000 pounds of grapes per year. On an interesting note, the Hubers even made their oak barrels from their very own white oak trees and fermented their 1999 estate vintage red wines in these barrels. I guess you can say that these wines were produced from estate oak and grapes.

Ted and Greg Huber run the orchard and winery, but Ted is the master winemaker. He gives his father, Gerald, most of the credit for teaching him the trade. Ted started out as a helping hand when he was 12 years old by bottling the wine, which was all done by hand! Gerald was the first commercial winemaker in the family and he, like his son, took classes at Ohio State University on the art of winemaking. By the time Ted was a teenager, both he and his father were Huber's master winemakers.

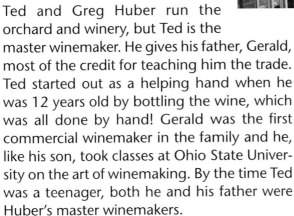

The Huber Winery has an underground cellar next to the barn (gift shop). The farmer's market is as big as a supermarket, but with personality and estate-grown fruit and vegetables. They also have a bakery with fresh baked breads and cookies to munch on. After your wine tour in the cellar, go to the Huber Starlight Inn next to the barn. The Inn has both indoor and outdoor seating. Weather permitting, sit outdoors, because it overlooks one of the most beautiful Indiana estates.

The Huber Winery offers 15 different varieties of grape wines such as Seyval Blanc, Vidal, Chancellor and Vignoles. The strong wines here are: the Huber Family Reserve; the White Blossom—a smoky, sur lie dry wine—barrel fermented, aged in oak and made to perfection; and the dynamite Heritage wine, made from Chambourcin

grapes—complex, full of cherry and raspberry and a hint of fig flavors—a very appealing wine. Since these bottles sell out very quickly,

the reserve wines are not always available for wine tasting. For softer wines, Huber makes a semi-sweet Starlite White, a flowery and app-ley wine with an oak aftertaste–a wine that is consistently delicious. Something different on Huber's wine menu is the Ice wine. Weather depending, this wine is only available for a couple of months out of the year.

They are presently expanding their acreage of vineyard and will be planting Cabernet Franc, Lemberger, Sauvignon and many other vari-eties. Actually, since the 1980s, the Hubers, in collaboration with the Indiana Wine and Grape Council, have been experimenting with Vitis vinifera grapes in their vineyard. They are watching for diseases, trying to obtain more extensive knowledge of the soil for the grapes and deciding how to manipu-late Mother Nature. Since the Hubers have been growing peaches, a very delicate fruit, they felt that they could grow the delicate vinifera grape as well. However, you won't be seeing Cabernet Sauvignon labels from the Hubers–they are growing viniferas to blend with their existing grapes. As Ted explains, he is very much into the art of wine blending.

Huber Orchard and Winery

19816 Huber Road
Starlight, IN 47106
Phone: (812) 923-WINE or
(800) 345-WINE
Fax: (812) 923-3013

www.Huberwinery.com
Email: info@huberwinery.com

Open:
Mon–Sat: 9am–6pm
Sun: 10am–6pm

Kauffman Winery

Kauffman Winery is located in Mt. Vernon on Old Lower Mt. Vernon Road. It is the only Southwestern Indiana winery. This winery does not have regular scheduled hours for tasting and touring. You must call ahead to see if they can accommodate you. However, the winery will ship their wine to you.

Harley and Bettye Kauffman were among the first wine grape growers to plant their vineyards in 1974. They started the vineyard to supply another winery with grapes, but that winery went out of business and Harley and Bettye were left with a full-grown vineyard and a ton of grapes. Harley, a resourceful man, taught himself how to make wine and soon started producing estate wines. Harley has a well-deserved reputation in the industry as an excellent winemaker and he still supplies many new and old wineries with grapes. Winemakers have won many medals with grapes from this vineyard. They are not a retail winery—they make and sell wine wholesale only.

Harley's focus is on balanced wines using hybrids and native American grapes. His Kauffman 76, a '99 Vintage Concord, won the prestigious Gold at the Indy International Wine Competition.

Kauffman Winery
9901 Old Lower Mt. Vernon Road
Mt.Vernon, IN 47620
Phone: (812) 985-3145
Call ahead for hours.

Turtle Run Winery and Vineyard

Opening March/April of 2001

From Huber's Winery, go south on Dow Knob Road toward St. Johns Road by turning right. Dow Knob Road becomes Engle Road, then Scottsville Road. Turn right onto Navilleton Road, then turn left onto Steiller Road and finally, turn left onto US-150. Take the I-64 West/IN-62 West ramp. Merge onto I-64 West/IN-62 West. Stay straight and take Exit 113 toward Lanesville, then veer left at the fork in the ramp. Turn left onto Lanesville Road/Old Lanesville Road and turn right onto IN-62. Turn left onto St. Peters Church Road. You will see a barn with a sign saying Turtle Run Winery. It takes about 1-1/2 hours to get from Huber's to Turtle Run.

Jim and Laura Pfeiffer own the Turtle Run Winery and Vineyard. They started this venture in 1997, after a couple years of producing great wines and visiting several Indiana wineries. They spent the next three years searching for the perfect place to set up a vineyard and winery.  Their search started out in Kentucky, but they found that the laws for winemaking were not developed and the land was too dry and expensive. They finally settled in Southern Indiana, a perfect place for wine grape growing. Between 1998-2000, they planted eight acres of Chambourcin, Vignoles, Traminettes and Chardonel. They don't plan to stop their expansion of growth until they have 65 acres and a full estate winery. To add to their wine production, they also buy grapes from around the U.S. for their Zinfindel and Chardonel.

The winery opens March 2001, with their first harvest of Vignoles and Chambourcin. I can't wait to try their wine.

Turtle Run Winery

940 St. Peters Church Road NE
Corydon, IN 47112
Phone: (866) 288-7853

Hours:

Sat: 10am–6pm
Sun: Noon–5pm

Winzerwald Winery and Vineyard

From Turtle Run Winery, head south for another new and wonderful startup, the Winzerwald Winery and Vineyard. Start out going northeast on St. Peters Church Road. Turn right onto IN-62. Turn left onto Crandall Lanesville Road, which soon becomes Lanesville Road and then turn left to take the I-64 West ramp. I-64 West merges with IN-37 South, so be careful to stay on I-64 West to IN-145, Exit number 72, toward Bristow/Birdseye. Go left at the fork in the ramp and take IN-145 all the way to the winery.

Dan and Donna Adams own the Winzerwald Winery, which opens in the spring of 2001. They have 82 acres of beautiful rolling hills in the Hoosier National Forest in Perry County.

The surrounding stately trees stand tall and at attention, ready to protect the vineyards from the harsh Indiana winters. This is the perfect place for Winzerwald Winery.

The Adams have a nontraditional set-up. They are both certified from Purdue University in viticulture and enology. They are both good winemakers. They have been growing grapes for years and selling them on the open market to other wineries. However, when wine made from their grapes started winning awards, they decided to make their own wine from their estate.

It's a good thing, too, because the Adams won Best Indiana and Best National Amateur wine awards in 1998 from the Indy International Wine Competition, the first time anyone in Indiana won the national honors. It was with a wine made from grapes brought to America from Germany by Dan's ancestors. The grape is unidentifiable and so the Adams named it "mystery grape".

Their vineyards currently have French-American hybrids such as Marechal Foch, Vignoles and Traminette. They plan to plant more German varieties in the immediate future, such as the Riesling and Lemberger and, of course, the mystery grape.

Winzerwald Winery
26300 North Indian Lake Road
Bristow, IN 47515

N

Chateau Pomije
Winery & Restaurant

Villa Milan Winery

Madison Vineyards
Lanthier Winery & Tasting Room

The Ridge Winery

The Thomas Family Winery

This is the second tour for Southern Indiana. This tour is around historical Madison and the Ohio River Valley. On this tour is the Lanthier Winery, Thomas Family Winery, Madison, Villa Milan, Chateau Pomije and the Ridge Winery.

Villa Milan Vineyard

Lanthier Winery and Tasting Room

There are two locations in Madison for Lanthier: the tasting room on Main Street and their winery/restaurant on Mill Street. From Indianapolis, take I-65 South to US 31 (Exit 76). Go southeast on US 31, passing Columbus to SR 7 south. Stay on SR 7 to SR 56. Travel east on SR 56 to US 421. Go south on US 421 to downtown Madison. Turn right on Main Street. The winery is on the right.

Lanthier Winery was the first to set up in Madison and is owned by Chris Lanthier and Tami Hagemeir. Chris and Tami decided to open a winery after a long vacation in Napa Valley. Chris, as a chemical engineer, knew he had the right background to make a fine cellarmaster. They bought a very unusual building in 1992, and spent two years cleaning up the grounds. The building has three different architectural structures: the guest house is an 1850s quaint, red brick building. The center wine tasting room was a fort built in the 1750s, and the wine production room was built in the 1940s as a scrap metal recycling plant. It is quite an interesting building to see. The interior is decorated uniquely as well, with the upstairs done in vintage 1960s and the downstairs lined with Lanthier bottles of wine and statues draped in fine silks.

Chris Lanthier is the cellarmaster and Tami Hagemeir manages the restaurant, tasting

rooms and the gardens. They released their first bottles of wine in the fall of 1994 and by December of that year, they had sold all 2,500 bottles.

In 1999 Chris began growing wine grapes and bought six acres of land for their vineyard. They are presently growing Chardonel, Cabernet Sauvignon, Merlot and Traminette.

A must try among the drier wines is the Rivertown White, a wine with a grassy, herbaceous aroma and flavor. Chris' oak-aged Cabernet Sauvignon is a top-quality red wine, full of the rich fruit flavors of black cherry and raspberry combined with an aftertaste of cedar and bell peppers. For an off-dry wine, try the delicious Rifleport Red. From their vineyards, watch for the Traminette and the Chardonel, which should be released by 2002.

The locals like their off-dry and sweet wines, both of which Lanthier Winery makes plenty of. The most popular wine is the Mill Street Red, which is a sweet, grape-flavored wine. Enjoy it for dessert.

Lanthier Winery

123 Mill Street
Madison, IN 47250
Phone: (812) 273-2409
(800) 41-WINES
Fax: (812) 273-5370

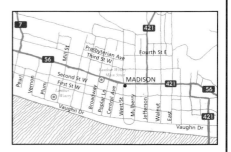

Lanthier Tasting Room

112 East Main Street
Madison, IN 47250
Phone: (812) 273-6678

Open:
Wed–Sun: 11am–5pm
Sat: 11am–8pm

The Thomas Family Winery

This winery is just a couple of blocks from Lanthier Winery. Go toward the Ohio River to Second Street and look for the sign.

Steve Thomas, the eldest son of eight, learned his trade as a winemaker from his father, Dr. Charlie Thomas, of the Chateau Thomas Winery in Indianapolis. He began making home wines with his father as a teenager. He did everything from washing bottles to making the wine. After four years at Ball State University, Steve went to work with his father as a winemaker for 10 years. By 1993, he and his wife, Elizabeth, set out to open their own winery in historic Madison. They opened their doors for wine tasting on Halloween night in 1995.

They bought a rehabilitated 1850s stable and carriage house to serve as their home and the winery. The winery resembles an Old World pub. Steve, Elizabeth and their two children live on the top floor, while the winery and production rooms are on the first floor. The winery has kept the flavor of the carriage house with dark wood and brick walls, high beams and rustic wooden picnic tables with benches. The Thomases built the winery with the idea that wine is a fun and enjoyable drink. They offer a variety of cheeses, salamis and crusted bread to eat with the wine. Every Saturday night, you will find a band playing at winery. They even make "Thomas Family Winery Live" CDs. The music is true Old World music such as Celtic, Bluegrass, Americana, Jazz and Blues. This winery is a really fun place to be.

Their latest venture is a partnership with a neighboring orchard. They are growing their

own apples for their Gale's Hard Cider (from Steve's paternal grandfather's recipe). This is a best-seller and a must-try. If you open the bottle, you have to drink it that day. It is a strong, dry drink and is just wonderful!

Another surprise from this winery is that they make their cherry and Concord wines in the dry French style, which is very unique, quite delicious and far from a dessert wine. If you like dry red wines, the must-try is the Rio Red with fruity characteristics of cherries and strawberries. A couple of red wines to watch for are the Zinfandel and the Shiraz—they make their debut in the fall of 2001.

Thomas Family Winery

208 East Second Street
Madison, IN 47250
Phone: (812) 273-3755
(800) 948-8466

www.thomasfamilywinery.com

Open:
Mon–Thurs: 11am–6pm
Fri–Sat: 11am–9pm
Sun: Noon–5pm

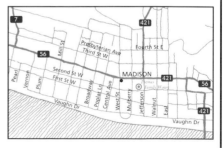

Madison Vineyards

From the Thomas Family Winery, head to to the Madison Winery and Vineyards. This is one of the few vineyards that has a winery at the entrance. From Madison, take US-421 North. Go to CR-400 North and turn right–you can't miss it because there are signs posted telling you how to get there. Turn on the dirt road and go past the vineyard to the winery.

Steve and Sandy Palmer own this winery. Steve, the master winemaker, dabbled with homemade wines for many years. Sandy bought Steve a winemaking kit for Christmas the first year they were married, 29 years ago. They opened Madison Vineyards in 1996. The winery does a large volume in sales, and those who go to the winery never leave empty-handed. Their tasting room is quaint and the back veranda overlooks the luscious green rolling hills of the vineyard.

In 1994, Steve and Sandy bought a 37-acre cattle farm for their vineyard and winery. The winery sits on a hill from which you can see all

the surrounding farmlands. You literally walk right into their vineyards when you visit the winery. Take a walk through these grapevines with Steve, and sampling the wine afterwards will take on a whole new meaning. The Palmers have planted 10 acres of the northeastern United States grape varieties–Vitis labrusca, Vitis vinifera and the French-American hybrids. Using the viniferas, Steve plans to make a Meritage–a blend of classic Bordeaux grapes.They are only the second winery to make this in Indiana.

During the spring of 2000, they planted Cabernet Sauvignon, Merlot and Petit Verdot. There will be additional planting in the year 2001, such as a clone of the Cabernet Sauvignon and a block of the Cabernet Franc. Steve's Petit Blanc is one of the best white wines that I have ever tasted. With delicate melon and lemon flavors, it's crisp and clean on the palate. Steve's estate Marechal Foch, aged in Hungarian oak barrels, is a young and spicy red, full of black currant flavors. Steve's future plan is to have all of Madison's wines become estate-grown grape wines, processed and bottled at Madison Vineyards. The Palmers have many activities planned around the summer and harvest season. For example, they have "The Blue Pig" hog roast with live music in July. There is also the Harvest Hoot, which is a harvest celebration that takes place in September.

Madison Vineyards

1456 East 400 North
Madison, IN 47250
Phone: (812) 273-6500
(888) 473-6500

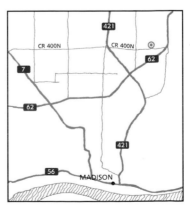

Villa Milan Winery

From Madison, head to Villa Milan Winery. Head toward Versailles on US-421 North. Go east on US-50 to IN-101 North toward Milan. Turn left onto IN-350. Turn right on County Road 50 North and you will see the winery driveway.

In 1977, John and Dot Garrett bought property in Ripley County. One year later, they began planting their vineyard. After harvesting their grapes, they would sell them to home winemakers and wineries. By 1984, they had built their own winery and in 1986, Villa Milan's first vintage, Vino di John, was released. They now have additional wines that they sell at the winery such as Vidal, Catawba and the Concord. This winery does not produce a large variety of wines, however, their winery is well worth the visit.

Their vineyard is breathtaking. It sits atop rolling hills drenched in brilliant sunlight. They have a thirty-two-foot gazebo that overlooks the vineyard and serves as a perfect place for a glass of wine. The winery has a restaurant with a full-service menu that is more like an Italian restaurant you would find in Milan, Italy. The restaurant serves everything from Manicotti to an Italian sausage dinner. Dot makes homemade hard rolls to complement John's wine. I highly recommend trying one. For lunch, you can get a sandwich with one of Dot's hard rolls. Eat lunch out on the gazebo with a glass of Vino di John and take in the glimmering hues of the sunlight that bathes the vineyard.

Villa Milan Winery

7287 East County Road 50 North
P.O. Box 248
Milan, IN 47031
Phone: (812) 654-3419

Email: villamil@seidata.com
www.seidata.com/villa-milan

Call for hours.

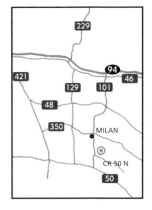

Chateau Pomije Winery and Restaurant

From Villa Milan Winery, go east on IN-350 by turning right, then turn left onto IN-101 and then right onto Eastern Avenue (this becomes CR-1100 North). Turn right onto West Country Line Road and then left onto North Dearborn Road.

Chateau Pomije is a Shumrick family-owned estate winery that got its start in 1973. They bought two acres in the Ohio River Valley and planted French-American hybrids. (They now have 40 acres of hybrids and 18 acres of vinifera.) By 1986, the Shumricks were ready to open a winery and restaurant.

Their turn-of-the-century stone-face winery sits in the middle of their gorgeous 100 acres of endless rolling hills flanked by vineyards. The winery interior is all natural wood complemented by stone walls. There are few wineries like this in Indiana. The winery has a first class restaurant, which is housed in the reconstructed 100-year-old timber barn. The main attraction in the restaurant is not just the food, but also the oversized stone fireplace–the largest in Indiana. There are large picture windows that allow you to take in the beautiful, majestic scenery of acres of glimmering red and white grapes. You can also view this scene

from their veranda that is just outside of the restaurant. If you visit during the peak of fall foliage you will be able to see the rainbow of brilliant purple, lemon and cranberry colors as the leaves turn.

Jerry Shumrick is the master winemaker and proprietor of the winery. Shumrick makes classic French vinifera wines such as the Cabernet Sauvignon and Merlot. Shumrick's estate-bottled Pinot Noir is a must try– it's full-bodied and filled with ripe, deep fruit. One of their best is the 1997 estate-bottled Riesling.

The Indiana winery is not their only enterprise. The Shumricks also have O'Bryonville Café and Wine Store in Cincinnati, Ohio. They are partners with two wineries in California: Tobin James (owned by a Shumrick) and Eberle Winery.

Chateau Pomije

25060 Jacobs Road
Guilford, IN 47022
Phone: (812) 623-3332
(800) 791-WINE
Fax: (812) 623-2489

www.chatpom.com

Open:
Tues–Thurs & Sun: Noon–8pm
Fri–Sat: 12pm–10pm

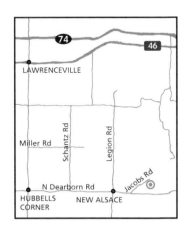

The Ridge Winery

The Ridge Winery is located at 227 Park Ridge in Vevay. The winery is not open for tours or wine tasting. They make wine and sell it at local establishments, and you can also order direct from Ridge Winery.

Tom and Mary Demaree opened the winery in 1995. Tom is the winery's full-time winemaker and Mary is the president. They produce and bottle all of their wines on the premises and sell them for dine-in or carry-out in Vevey at Ogle Haus Inn, IGA Grocery, Steamboat Liquors, Roxano's Restaurant, Cuz's Bar, T&J Market and L&L Kwik Stop.

Currently, they make and sell Concord and Blackberry sweet wines. Their sweet wines are anything but syrupy. The Blackberry is a delicious smooth and crisp wine–a delightful afternoon drink. For their semi-dry they have Country White and Country Red. These wines are not Merlots, but if you like wines that don't have the acidity and are low in tannin, these are great. Tom buys the juice from around the U.S., but mostly from Indiana vineyards. The winery's average production is around 3,000 bottles a year. Their future plans are to have their own vineyard and open a winery in the town of Vevay.

Ridge Winery
227 Park Ridge
Vevay, IN 47043

Southern Indiana Wineries and Their Communities

Information

Madison/Jefferson County Convention and Visitors Bureau
301 E. Main Street
(812) 265-2956 or
(800) 559-2956
Thomas Family Winery, Lanthier Winery, Madison Vineyards

Dearborn County Convention, Recreation and Visitors Bureau
790 Rudolph Way
(812) 537-0814 or
(800) 322-8198
Chateau Pomije

Orange County Tourism Commission
P.O. Box 150
(877) 422-9925
French Lick Winery

Harrison County Chamber of Commerce
310 N. Elm Street
(812) 738-2137 or
(888) 738-2137
Huber Orchard and Winery

Ripley County Convention, Recreation and Visitors Commission
133 N. Main Street
(812) 689-6654
Villa Milan Winery

Places to Eat

Nex-Dor Restaurant and Lounge
700 Clifty Drive
Madison, IN
(812) 273-5151

The Wharf Restaurant and Lounge
On the Riverfront at Broadway
Madison, IN
(812) 265-2688

Zeppelin's Deli
719 W. Main Street
(812) 265-DELI

Milan Railroad Inn
Main and Carr Streets
(812) 654-2800 or
(800) 448-7405

Taverne on the Lake
19325 Schmarr Drive
Lawrenceburg, IN
(812) 537-9000

Chicago's Pizza
Highway 56
French Lick, IN
(812) 936-2962

Marsha's Uptown Café
156 S. Maple Street
Orleans, IN
(812) 865-1535

The Mineral Spring
124 SE Court Street
Paoli, IN
(812) 723-4648

Cracker Barrel
2393 Pacer Court NW
Corydon, IN
(812) 734-0407

Magdalena's Family Restaurant
103 E. Chestnut Street
Corydon, IN
(812) 738-8075

Ryan's Steak House
2230 Edsel Lane
Corydon, IN
(812) 734-0025

Places to Stay

Clifty Inn, Clifty Falls State Park
1501 Green Road
Madison, IN
(812) 265-4135

Roth's Get-Away Cottages
203 Walnut Street
Madison, IN
(812) 265-6636

Vintage Views Inn
411 W. First Street
Madison, IN
(812) 265-6856
www.vintageviewsinn.com

Milan Railroad Inn
Main and Carr Streets
Milan, IN
(812) 654-2800 or
(800) 448-7405

Wilstem Guest Ranch
P.O. Box 88
French Lick, IN
(812) 936-4484
You should definitely check this place out—it offers a variety of unique amenities!

French Lick Springs Villas
French Lick, IN
(812) 936-5000 or
(800) 522-9210
Perfect for families!

Kintner House Inn
Capitol Avenue and
Chestnut Street
Corydon, IN
(812) 738-2020

Baymont Inn
Landmark Avenue at
State Road 135
Corydon, IN
(812) 738-1500 or
(800) 428-3438

Sights to See

Lanier Mansion
511 W. First Street
Madison, IN
(812) 265-3526
Originally owned by James Lanier, this 1840s mansion is still decorated according to the time period in which it was built. The 3-story spiral staircase just adds to the fairy tale quality of the house.

Clifty Falls State Park
1501 Green Road
Madison, IN
(812) 265-1331
With 1,360 acres of breathtaking beauty, this park is also home to the Clifty Canyon State Nature Preserve. This very deep canyon can only be reached on foot, but the hike is magnificent. There is plenty of lush vegetation and in the spring, there are flowing waterfalls. The park also has a swimming pool, nature center and a campground.

Hillforest Mansion
213 Fifth Street
Aurora, IN
(812) 926-0087
This mansion, originally owned by Thomas Gaff, was built in the 1850s. The style is often referred to as "steamboat gothic," because its characteristics match that of a steamboat. The house is now filled with antiques and is available for tours. See everything from the wine cellar to the observatory upstairs.

Red Wolf Sanctuary
P.O. Box 23
Lawrenceburg, IN
(812) 667-5303
(please set appointment)
Paul and Jane Strasser developed this sanctuary in order to help animals that are injured or sick. Right now, they have gray and red wolves, a mountain lion, foxes, coyotes and several raptors. The

red wolves are hybrids, since red wolves are now extinct in the wild. The Strassers use their 23 acres to nurse animals back to health and then release them into the wild when they are ready. However, some of the animals never fully recover. Those are the ones who make the sanctuary their new home.

Indiana Railway Museum
P.O. Box 150
French Lick, IN
(812) 936-2405 or
(800) 74-TRAIN

Take a ride through the Hoosier National Forest and then through the 2,200-foot-long Burton Tunnel. You can also schedule to be on the train during one of their re-enactments of a "Wild West Hold-Up."

Ski and Snowboard Paoli Peaks
P.O. Box 67
Paoli, IN
(812) 723-4696

Be prepared for giant jumps and moguls, a quarter-pipe and plenty of snow ramps. Midnight packages are also available.

Bluespring Caverns–
Mystery River Voyage
RR 11, Box 1245
(812) 279-9471

Take a tour down a river in the caverns. See rare blind fish and crayfish. When you finish, have lunch in the picnic area, browse the gift shop or prospect for gold and gems.

Squire Boone Caverns
P.O. Box 411
Mauckport, IN
(812) 732-4381 or
(502) 425-2283

See everything from streams, waterfalls, cave crickets, blind fish and crayfish and maybe even some bats–all underground! These caverns are also home to the world's largest travertine dam formation. Halfway through your tour, there is a

complete blackout in the cave. Once outside the caverns, you can enjoy the craft shops, homemade candy store and restaurant, which are housed in the log cabins. There is also a petting zoo, fossil dig and gem panning for kids.

Zimmerman Art Glass Factory
395 Valley Road NW
Corydon, IN
(812) 738-2206

Run by brothers Bart and Kerry Zimmerman, you can come here to see the brothers hand blow glass pieces. They will make just about anything upon request, but their specialties are paperweights and clear crystal balls, which house flower blossoms.

INDIANA WINERIES

Lake Michigan Winery

Whiting White

TABLE WINE   CONTAINS SULFITES
Produced and Bottled by: Lake Michigan Winery
U.S. 41 "Calumet Av." At 119th St., Whiting, In. 46394
Ph. 219-659-WINE & Fax 219-659-3501
GRAPE IDEA@AOL.COM

 3

Lanthier Winery

Premier
Blush
Limited Cellar Release
Semi-Sweet Table Wine

Produced & Bottled By Lanthier Winery
Madison, Indiana
47250 · U.S.A.

750 ML.   Serve
CONTAINS SULFITES   Lightly Chilled

22

MADISON
Vineyards

1997 Estate
Seyval Blanc
Ohio River Valley Table Wine
Produced and Bottled by Madison Vineyards, Inc., Madison, IN 47250

24

O · L · I · V · E · R

DRY GEWÜRZTRAMINER
PRODUCED AND BOTTLED BY OLIVER WINERY, BLOOMINGTON, INDIANA
ALCOHOL 12% BY VOLUME

 11

Thomas Family Winery

Vidal Blanc 1996

PRODUCED AND BOTTLED BY THE THOMAS FAMILY WINERY, INC. IN MADISON, IN
BW-IN-36 FOR SALE IN INDIANA ONLY 11% ALCOHOL BY VOLUME

 23

NORTHERN INDIANA
1. Anderson Orchard and Winery
2. Dune Ridge Winery
3. Lake Michigan Winery
4. Satek Winery

CENTRAL INDIANA
5. Easley Winery
6. Gaia Winery
7. Chateau Thomas Winery
8. Terre Vin Winery
9. Ferrin's Fruit Winery
10. Wilson Winery

SOUTH CENTRAL INDIANA
11. Oliver Winery and Vineyard
12. Butler Winery
13. Brown County Winery
14. Chateau Thomas Tasting Room
15. Simmons Winery
16. Shadey Lake Winery

SOUTHERN INDIANA
17. French Lick Winery
18. Huber Orchard and Winery
19. Turtle Run Winery and Orchard
20. Winzerwald Winery and Vineyard
21. Kauffman Winery

SOUTHERN INDIANA-EAST
22. Lanthier Winery and Tasting Room
23. The Thomas Family Winery
24. Madison Vineyards
25. Villa Milan Winery
26. Chateau Pomije Winery and Restaurant
27. The Ridge Winery

VILLA MILAN
Concord
OHIO RIVER VALLEY
RED TABLE WINE

PRODUCED AND BOTTLED BY
Villa Milan Vineyard

MILAN, IND. 47031   CONTAINS SULFITES

25